FABULOUS
FRACTIONS

Magical Math

FABULOUS
FRACTIONS

Games and Activities
That Make Math Easy and Fun

Lynette Long

John Wiley & Sons, Inc.

New York • Chichester • Weinheim • Brisbane • Singapore • Toronto

Published by John Wiley & Sons, Inc.
Published simultaneously in Canada

Design and production by Navta Associates, Inc.

The Publisher and the author have made every reasonable effort to ensure that the experiments and activities in this book are safe when conducted as instructed but assume no responsibility for any damage caused or sustained while performing the experiments or activities in the book. Parents, guardians, and/or teachers should supervise young readers who undertake the experiments and activities in this book.

Library of Congress Cataloging-in-Publication Data:

Long, Lynette.
   Fabulous fractions : games and activities that make math easy and fun / Lynette Long.
      p. cm.—(Magical math)
   Includes index.
   ISBN 0-471-36981-0 (pbk.)
      1. Fractions—Juvenile literature. [1. Fractions.] I. Title.

   QA117 .L66 2001
   513.2'6—dc21   00-043386

Printed in the United States of America

10 9 8 7 6 5 4 3 2 1

Contents

THE MAGIC OF FRACTIONS

The world is full of fractions. If there weren't any fractions, you couldn't have half of your friend's cookie, or leave one-third of your spinach on your plate, or eat one-eighth of a pizza. What if your father sent you to the market to pick up a few groceries? On the list he might write:

- ¼ pound of American cheese

- ¾ pound of ham

- ½ gallon of milk

- half a dozen eggs

- one loaf of bread

If there weren't any fractions, you'd have to get either a whole of everything or nothing. Neither of these options would make your dad very happy.

What are fractions? "Fractions" are just another way to write numbers. Fractions show that a number is part of a set. For example, if you ate one slice of pizza out of an eight-slice pie, you can show that in a fraction by saying that you ate one-eighth (⅛) of the pizza. The word *fraction* means "part of a whole," from the Latin *fractio*, meaning "to break into pieces."

A fraction has two parts, a "numerator" and a "denominator." The numerator and the denominator are separated by a bar, as in $\frac{1}{2}$, or a slant line, as in ½ or 1/2 . The numerator is written on top of the bar or to the left of the slant line, and the denominator is written below the bar or to the right of the slant line. However the fraction is written, one-half means one of two equal parts of a whole. Look at the parts of these fractions:

- In the fraction $\frac{3}{4}$, 3 is the numerator and 4 is the denominator.

- In the fraction ⅔, 2 is the numerator and 3 is the denominator.

- In the fraction 1/10, 1 is the numerator and 10 is the denominator.

- In the fraction ⁴⁄₃, 4 is the numerator and 3 is the denominator.

The denominator tells you how many equal parts make up the whole. If the denominator is 4, the whole is divided into four equal parts. If the denominator is 3, the whole is divided into three equal parts. The numerator represents how many parts are being used. If the numerator is 2, two parts are being used. If the numerator is 1, one part is being used.

Fractions can be expressed in words, such as "I'd like half a sandwich" for $\frac{1}{2}$ or "I'll be back in a quarter of an hour" for $\frac{1}{4}$. For most fractions, the word is just a combination of the numerator and the denominator, so $\frac{1}{6}$ is said as "one-sixth."

FRACTION WORDS

Number Forms	Word Forms
$\frac{1}{2}$	one-half or half
$\frac{1}{4}$	one-fourth or one quarter
$1\frac{1}{2}$	one and a half
$\frac{13}{16}$	thirteen-sixteenths

If you want to eat one-fourth of a sandwich, first divide the sandwich into four equal parts, and then eat one of them: $\frac{1}{4}$.

If you want to eat three-fourths of an apple, first divide the apple into four equal parts, and then eat three of them: $\frac{3}{4}$.

If you want to drink half a glass of milk, first mentally divide the milk in the glass into two equal parts, and then drink one of them: $\frac{1}{2}$.

Fractions are an essential mathematical skill. You will use fractions every day of your life, so start practicing with the 40 fun fraction activities in this book. After the first one, you will have done one-fortieth of the activities. After the last one, you'll be a fractions master. Then you can proudly display the fractions master certificate at the back of this book.

~~~ II ~~~
THE FACTS ON FRACTIONS

In this section, you'll learn everything you need to know about fractions, starting with what fractions look like and how to write them. You'll learn about halves, quarters, and more complex fractions. You'll also be able to reduce fractions, change a mixed number to an improper fraction and vice versa, and create equivalent fractions.

While you're learning, you'll be making sandwiches, cutting up imaginary pizzas, constructing number lines, testing your psychic powers, and playing games of speed and skill. Once you've finished the 13 chapters in this section, the rest of the book should be a piece of cake—27/40 to be exact!

Half Happenings

Explore some different ways to make one-half.

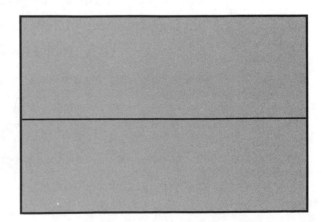

MATERIALS

3 or more pieces of construction paper in different colors

scissors

Procedure

1. Fold a piece of construction paper in half lengthwise. Cut the paper in half on the fold. Each of these pieces is exactly the same size. Each piece is one-half of the original piece of paper.

2. Fold another piece of construction paper in half the other way. Cut the paper in half on the fold. Each of these pieces is exactly the same size. Each piece is one-half of the original piece of paper.

3. Fold another piece of construction paper in half diagonally. Cut the paper in half on the fold. Each of these pieces is exactly the same size. Each piece is one-half of the original piece of paper.

4. There are lots of ways to cut a piece of construction paper in half. How many ways can you find?

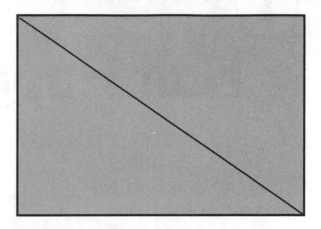

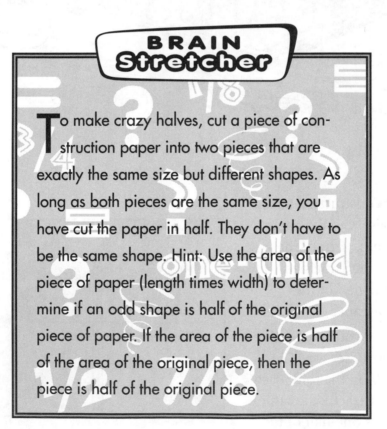

BRAIN Stretcher

To make crazy halves, cut a piece of construction paper into two pieces that are exactly the same size but different shapes. As long as both pieces are the same size, you have cut the paper in half. They don't have to be the same shape. Hint: Use the area of the piece of paper (length times width) to determine if an odd shape is half of the original piece of paper. If the area of the piece is half of the area of the original piece, then the piece is half of the original piece.

2

Sandwich Quarters

*How many ways can you cut a sandwich
into four equal parts?*

MATERIALS

8 slices of bread
sandwich fixings
knife
4 plates

Procedure

1. Make four sandwiches out of whatever you like. Put each sandwich on a plate.

2. Cut one of the sandwiches into four equal pieces by cutting it in half and in half again. It should look like the one shown. Each square piece is one-fourth of the whole sandwich.

3. Can you think of another way to cut a sandwich into four equal pieces? Cut the second sandwich along both diagonals as shown.

Each triangular piece is one-fourth of the whole sandwich.

4. Can you think of another way to cut a sandwich into four equal pieces? Cut a third sandwich into four long strips as shown.

Each long piece is one-fourth of the whole sandwich.

5. There is still another way to cut a sandwich into four equal pieces. Take the fourth sandwich and cut it first in half down the center. Then cut each of the halves in half again, using diagonal cuts as shown.

Each triangular piece is one-fourth of the whole sandwich.

6. Each of your four sandwiches is cut into four equal pieces in a different way. Even though they are different shapes, each of these pieces is one-fourth of the whole sandwich.

7. Make a whole sandwich by putting any four pieces together. For example, you can make a whole sandwich either of the two ways shown.

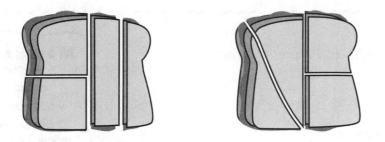

8. How many other ways can you make a whole sandwich using four pieces?

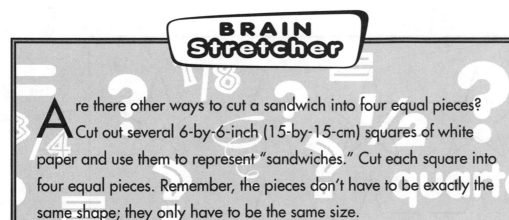

BRAIN Stretcher

Are there other ways to cut a sandwich into four equal pieces? Cut out several 6-by-6-inch (15-by-15-cm) squares of white paper and use them to represent "sandwiches." Cut each square into four equal pieces. Remember, the pieces don't have to be exactly the same shape; they only have to be the same size.

Fraction Stars

Learn how to write and represent fractions.

MATERIALS

pencil
white paper
3 crayons—
1 yellow, 1 orange,
and 1 green

Procedure

1. Draw eight stars on a piece of white paper as shown.

2. Color three of the stars yellow, two of the stars orange, and one of the stars green.

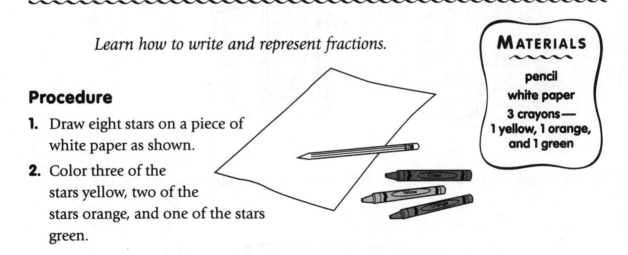

3. What fraction of the total number of stars is yellow? There are eight total stars and three of them are yellow, so three-eighths ($^3/_8$) of the stars are yellow.

4. What fraction of the total number of stars is orange? Two of the eight stars are orange, so two-eighths ($^2/_8$) of the stars are orange.

5. What fraction of the total number of stars is green? One of the eight stars is green, so one-eighth ($^1/_8$) of the stars are green.

6. What fraction of the total number of stars is still white? Two of the eight stars are white, so two-eighths ($^2/_8$) of the stars are white.

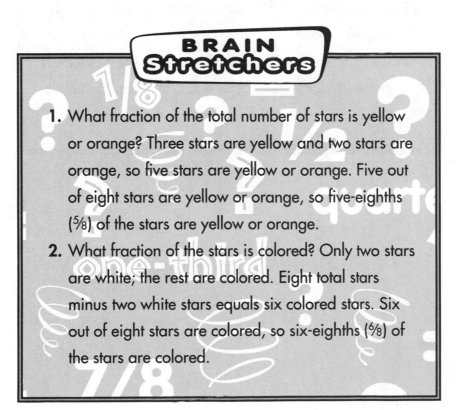

BRAIN Stretchers

1. What fraction of the total number of stars is yellow or orange? Three stars are yellow and two stars are orange, so five stars are yellow or orange. Five out of eight stars are yellow or orange, so five-eighths ($^5/_8$) of the stars are yellow or orange.

2. What fraction of the stars is colored? Only two stars are white; the rest are colored. Eight total stars minus two white stars equals six colored stars. Six out of eight stars are colored, so six-eighths ($^6/_8$) of the stars are colored.

SUPER BRAIN Stretchers

Get two rolls of assorted fruit-flavored candies. Open one roll and count the total number of pieces in the roll. Make a list of the number of pieces there are of each color.

1. What fraction of the total number of pieces is red?

2. What fraction of the total number of pieces is green? Yellow?

3. Open the other roll of candies and list the number of pieces of each color. Does each roll of candies have the same fraction of each color?

Fraction Strips

Equivalent fractions are fractions that have different numerators and denominators but the same value. Here's an easy way to learn about equivalent fractions.

MATERIALS

No. 2 pencil

piece of poster board

ruler

scissors

at least 9 different crayons or colored pencils

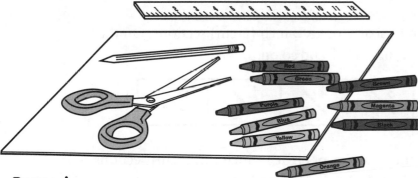

Procedure

1. Use a No. 2 pencil to draw nine strips on the poster board that are each 12 inches (30 cm) long and 1 inch (2.5 cm) wide. Cut out the strips.

2. Color each of the nine strips of poster board a different color.

3. On the first strip of poster board, write a 1. This strip represents one whole.

4. On the second strip, draw a line 6 inches (15 cm) from one end so that the strip is divided into halves, or two equal 6-inch (15-cm)-long sections. One the left half, write "1/2." On the right half, write "2/2."

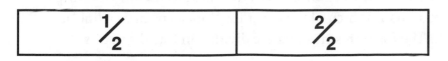

5. Divide the third strip into thirds, or three 4-inch (10-cm) sections. From left to right, write "1/3," "2/3," and "3/3" on the sections.

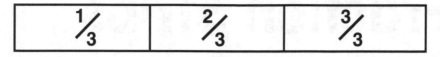

6. Divide the fourth strip into fourths, or four 3-inch (7.5-cm) sections. Write "1/4," "2/4," "3/4," and "4/4" on the sections.

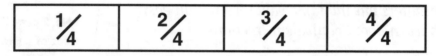

7. Divide the fifth strip into sixths, or six 2-inch (5-cm) sections. On the sections, write "1/6," "2/6," "3/6," and so on.

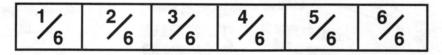

8. Divide the sixth strip into eighths, or eight $1\frac{1}{2}$-inch (3.75-cm) sections. On the sections, write "1/8," "2/8," "3/8," and so on.

9. Divide the seventh strip into ninths, or nine $1\frac{1}{3}$-inch (3.33 cm) sections. On the sections, write "1/9," "2/9," "3/9," and so on.

10. Divide the eighth strip into tenths, or ten $1\frac{1}{5}$-inch (3-cm) sections. On the sections, write "1/10," "2/10," "3/10," and so on.

11. Divide the ninth strip into twelfths, or twelve 1-inch (2.5-cm) sections. On the sections, write "1/12," "2/12," "3/12," and so on.

12. Now that you have made a set of fraction strips, you can use them to find equivalent fractions. For example, what other fractions are equal to 1/2? Line up each of the fraction strips in turn next to the fraction strip that is divided in half. Which of the other fraction strips have a line at the 1/2 mark? The fraction strips that are divided in fourths, sixths, eighths, tenths, and twelfths line up with the 1/2 mark, at 2/4, 3/6, 4/8, 5/10, and 6/12. These fractions are all equivalent to 1/2.

13. Use the fraction strips to find all the fractions that are equivalent to 1/3. Do any match?

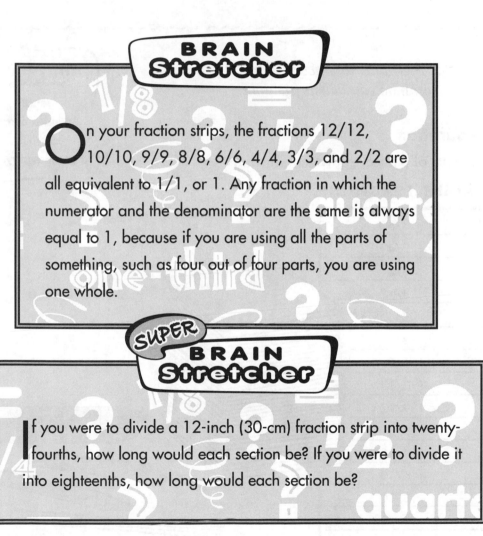

BRAIN Stretcher

On your fraction strips, the fractions 12/12, 10/10, 9/9, 8/8, 6/6, 4/4, 3/3, and 2/2 are all equivalent to 1/1, or 1. Any fraction in which the numerator and the denominator are the same is always equal to 1, because if you are using all the parts of something, such as four out of four parts, you are using one whole.

SUPER BRAIN Stretcher

If you were to divide a 12-inch (30-cm) fraction strip into twenty-fourths, how long would each section be? If you were to divide it into eighteenths, how long would each section be?

Fraction Match

Play this game to practice matching common equivalent fractions.

Game Preparation

1. Look at the list of pairs of equivalent fractions.

EQUIVALENT FRACTIONS

1/2	3/6
3/6	2/4
5/10	4/8
1/3	4/12
4/12	2/6
1/4	2/8
3/12	1/3
1/6	2/12
3/4	9/12
2/3	6/8
2/5	4/10
3/5	6/10
4/5	8/10
5/6	10/12
2/2	3/3
4/4	6/6
6/6	8/8

2. Write one of the fractions on each of 34 index cards, writing the number at the top of the card. On the back of the cards for the fractions listed in the right-hand column, write "E" for equivalent.

3. Below each fraction, draw a circle. Divide the circle into the number of pieces indicated in the denominator of the fraction. Use crayons to shade the number of pieces indicated in the numerator as shown.

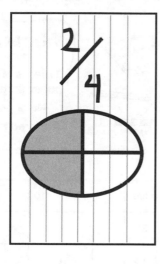
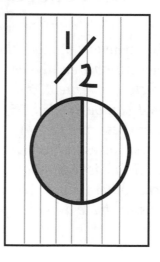

4. Separate the cards into two decks so that one of the decks contains only E cards.

Game Rules

1. Shuffle each deck of cards and place them all facedown on the table in two rows, one of cards with E's and one of cards without.

2. Player 1 turns over two cards, one from the E row and one from the other row. If the two cards show equivalent fractions, the player picks them up, puts them faceup in a pile on the table, and takes another turn. If the fractions on the two cards are not equivalent, the player places the cards facedown in their original position and player 2 takes a turn.

3. Play continues until all the pairs of equivalent fractions are found. The player with the most pairs of equivalent fractions wins the game.

Lowest-Terms Picture

A "factor" is any whole number that divides another number evenly. For example, the factors of 4 are 4, 2, and 1, because 4 can be divided evenly by each of these numbers. A fraction is in its "lowest terms" when the numerator and the denominator do not have a common factor other than 1. Use lowest-terms fractions to create a hidden picture.

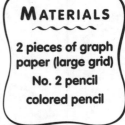

Procedure

1. Use the No. 2 pencil to outline a section of graph paper six squares long by six squares wide.

2. The following fractions are in lowest terms. Write them in the squares as shown so that they form a pattern. 5/6 3/8 1/2 2/3 11/12 5/8 3/4 9/10 5/6 1/6 4/5 1/3 1/4 2/5 3/7.

3. Fill in the remaining squares with the following fractions, which are not in lowest terms: 4/4 2/20 3/3 5/25 5/15 2/8 6/9 6/12 2/10 3/12 2/8 5/10 3/6 4/12 2/4 2/6 4/6 7/7 9/12 4/8 3/9.

5/6			9/10	5/6	3/7
3/8				1/6	
1/2				4/5	
2/3				1/3	
11/12				1/4	
5/8	3/4			2/5	

	4/4	2/8			
	2/20	6/9	5/10		4/6
	3/3	6/12	3/6		7/7
	5/25	2/10	4/12		9/12
	5/15	3/12	2/4		4/8
		2/8	2/6		3/9

4. Use a colored pencil to shade the fractions that are in lowest terms so that the hidden pattern is revealed.

5/6	4/4	2/8	9/10	5/6	3/7
3/8	2/20	6/9	5/10	1/6	4/6
1/2	3/3	6/12	3/6	4/5	7/7
2/3	5/25	2/10	4/12	1/3	9/12
11/12	5/15	3/12	2/4	1/4	4/8
5/8	3/4	2/8	2/6	2/5	3/9

5. Make up your own lowest-terms picture or pattern, using the Tips and Tricks box for help. Give your lowest-terms picture to a family member or friend and ask him or her to find the hidden picture.

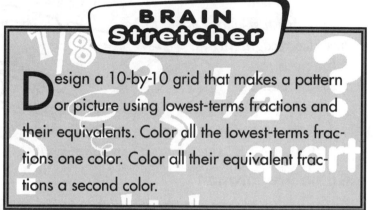

BRAIN Stretcher

Design a 10-by-10 grid that makes a pattern or picture using lowest-terms fractions and their equivalents. Color all the lowest-terms fractions one color. Color all their equivalent fractions a second color.

Tips and Tricks

To determine whether a fraction is in lowest terms, find the factors of the numerator and the denominator and see if they have any common factors other than 1.

For example, take the fraction 2/5. The factors of 2 are 1 and 2, and the factors of 5 are 1 and 5. The numerator and the denominator do not have any common factors other than 1. So 2/5 is in lowest terms.

Take the fraction 3/12. The factors of 3 are 1 and 3, and the factors of 12 are 1, 2, 3, 4, 6, and 12. Since 3 is a factor of both the numerator and the denominator, 3/12 is not in lowest terms. If you want to "reduce" 3/12 to lowest terms, divide both the numerator and the denominator by their common factor, 3: 3 ÷ 3 = 1 and 12 ÷ 3 = 4. The fraction 1/4 is in lowest terms. The two fractions 1/4 and 3/12 are also equivalent. Any fraction is equivalent to its reduced form.

Reduce It!

Play this fast-paced game to practice recognizing fractions that can be reduced.

MATERIALS

deck of playing cards

2 players

Game Preparation

Remove all the face cards (kings, queens, and jacks) from a deck of playing cards.

Game Rules

1. Shuffle the cards and deal each player 20 cards.

2. Each player places his or her cards facedown in a pile on the table.

3. Player 1 turns over the top card on his or her pile and places it faceup in the center of the table.

4. Player 2 turns over the top card in his or her pile and places it beside player 1's card. These two cards form a fraction in which the lower-value card is the numerator and the higher-value card is the denominator. Aces count as 1's. For example, if player 1 plays the 10 of diamonds and player 2 plays the 5 of spades, the fraction formed is 5/10.

5. Players quickly decide whether the fraction formed can be reduced. For example, 5/10 can be reduced because the numerator and the denominator share the common factor 5.

6. If the fraction formed can be reduced, players slap the cards and shout, "Reduce it!" The first player to correctly slap the cards wins the two cards and any other cards under them. If the player is incorrect, the other player wins the cards. The cards that each player wins are placed at the bottom of his or her pile to be played again later.

7. If the fraction formed by the two cards cannot be reduced and no one slaps it, the next player places another card on top of his or her old one and forms a new fraction.

8. Play continues until one player has won all the cards.

SUPER REDUCE IT!

Instead of shouting "Reduce it!" players reduce the fraction to lowest terms and shout the reduced fraction. For example, if the 4 of hearts and the 8 of spades are played to make the fraction 4/8, the player would slap the cards and shout, "One-half!"

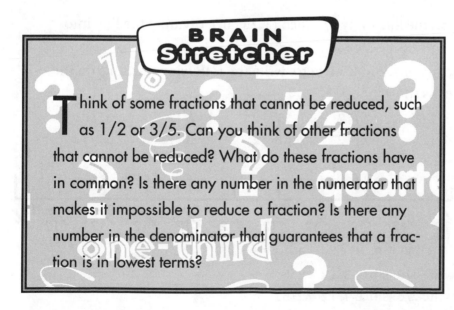

BRAIN Stretcher

Think of some fractions that cannot be reduced, such as 1/2 or 3/5. Can you think of other fractions that cannot be reduced? What do these fractions have in common? Is there any number in the numerator that makes it impossible to reduce a fraction? Is there any number in the denominator that guarantees that a fraction is in lowest terms?

8

The Lineup

Practice reducing equivalent fractions between 0 and 1.

Procedure

1. Draw a line 6 inches (15 cm) long on a piece of paper.

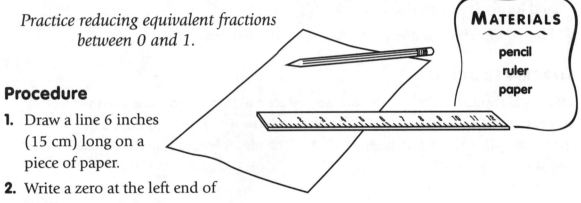

2. Write a zero at the left end of the line.

3. Place a mark on the line every 1/2 inch (1.25 cm), dividing the line into twelfths.

4. Starting at the first mark in from zero, write the following fractions on the marks in order as shown:

1/2	3/12	5/12	7/12	9/12	11/12
2/12	4/12	6/12	8/12	10/12	12/12

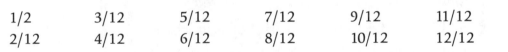

5. Write equivalent fractions in sixths as follows:

Under 2/12 write 1/6, since 2/12 = 1/6.
Under 4/12 write 2/6, since 4/12 = 2/6.
Under 6/12 write 3/6, since 6/12 = 3/6.

Under 8/12 write 4/6, since 8/12 = 4/6.
Under 10/12 write 5/6, since 10/12 = 5/6.
Under 12/12 write 6/6, since 12/12 = 6/6.

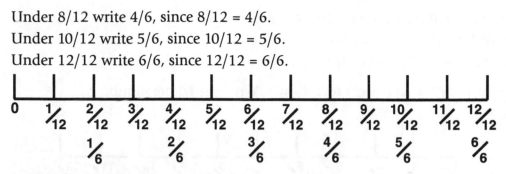

6. Write the equivalent fractions in fourths as follows:

Under 3/12 write 1/4, since 3/12 = 1/4.

Under 3/6 write 2/4, since 3/6 = 2/4.

Under 9/12 write 3/4, since 9/12 = 3/4.

Under 6/6 write 4/4, since 6/6 = 4/4.

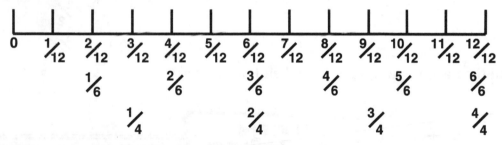

7. Write equivalent fractions in thirds as follows:

Under 2/6 write 1/3, since 2/6 = 1/3.

Under 4/6 write 2/3, since 4/6 = 2/3.

Under 4/4 write 3/3, since 4/4 = 3/3.

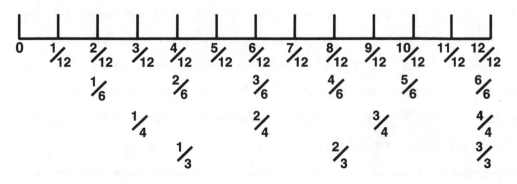

8. Write equivalent fractions in halves as follows:
   Under 2/4 write 1/2, since 2/4 = 1/2.
   Under 3/3 write 2/2, since 3/3 = 2/2.

9. The fraction 2/2 is equivalent to 1/1, or 1. Write the whole number 1/1 under 2/2.

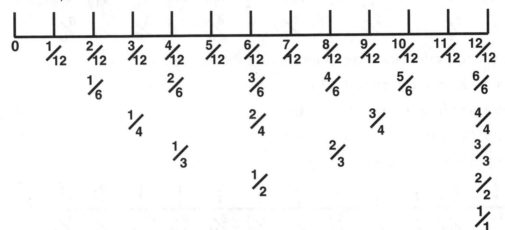

10. Are all the fractions now reduced to their lowest terms?

BRAIN Stretcher

How many fractions are there between 0 and 1? To figure it out, construct a fantasy fraction. Make 1 the numerator, then pick any whole number greater than 1 as the denominator. A "whole number" is any multiple of 1, and a "multiple" is a number that can be evenly divided by another number. The multiples of 1 are 1, 2, 3, and so on. Zero is also a whole number, but do not use it as the denominator of your fantasy fraction. Whatever whole number other than 0 or 1 that you pick as the denominator will create a fraction greater than 0 and less than 1. How many fantasy fractions can you create?

Fraction War!

Play this game to quickly recognize comparative values of fractions.

Game Preparation

Write one of the following fractions on each of 60 index cards.

1/1	1/5	1/8	1/9	1/10	1/12
1/2	2/5	2/8	2/9	2/10	2/12
2/2	3/5	3/8	3/9	3/10	3/12
1/3	4/5	4/8	4/9	4/10	4/12
2/3	5/5	5/8	5/9	5/10	5/12
3/3	1/6	6/8	6/9	6/10	6/12
1/4	2/6	7/8	7/9	7/10	7/12
2/4	3/6	8/8	8/9	8/10	8/12
3/4	4/6		9/9	9/10	9/12
4/4	5/6			10/10	10/12
	6/6				11/12
					12/12

Game Rules

1. Shuffle and deal the cards. Each player places his or her cards facedown in a pile in front of himself or herself.

2. Both players turn over their top card at the same time. The player whose card has the larger fraction wins both cards. Players can use a pencil and paper, and the Tips and Tricks box, to determine which fraction is larger.

3. If the players turn over equivalent fractions, there is a fraction war! Each player places three new cards facedown in a row and a fourth card faceup. The player whose faceup card has the larger fraction wins all eight cards plus the two played before the war.

4. The game continues until one player wins all the cards.

Tips and Tricks

• If two fractions have a common denominator (the same number in the denominator), the fraction with the larger numerator is the larger fraction. For example, 2/5 and 3/5 have a common denominator. Since 3 is greater than 2, 3/5 is larger than 2/5.

• If two fractions have a common numerator, the fraction with the smaller denominator is larger. For example, 1/3 and 1/4 have a common numerator, so 1/3 is larger since the denominator is smaller.

• If you are not sure which fraction is larger, convert both fractions to their lowest common denominator, then compare their numerators. The "lowest common denominator" is the smallest number that can be evenly divided by both denominators. For example, to

find the lowest common denominator of 3/5 and 5/12, multiply the denominators: $5 \times 12 = 60$. Can both denominators divide evenly a number lower than 60? They cannot. So 60 is the lowest common denominator. To convert the fractions, divide 60 by the denominator of each fraction: $60 \div 5 = 12$ for 3/5, and $60 \div 12 = 5$ for 5/12. Multiply each "quotient" (division answer) by the numerator of each fraction: $12 \times 3 = 36$ for 3/5, and $5 \times 5 = 25$ for 5/12. The "product" (multiplication answer) is the new numerator of each fraction, and 60 is the denominator. So 3/5 converts to 36/60, and 5/12 converts to 25/60. Which fraction is larger? The one with the larger numerator. Since 36 is larger than 25, 3/5 is larger than 5/12.

Domino ESP

Fractions can be "proper" or "improper." The value of a proper fraction is less than 1, and the value of an improper fraction is more than 1. Learn the difference between proper and improper fractions while you test your psychic powers.

Game Preparation

1. Write "Correct" on one piece of paper and "Incorrect" on another piece of paper.

2. Remove all the dominoes that are blank on one or both ends from the set.

3. Mix the remaining dominoes and place them facedown vertically in a horizontal row on the table.

Game Rules

1. Put your hand on the first domino on the left end of the row. Use your psychic powers to guess whether the dots on the other side of the domino represent a proper fraction or an improper fraction. The number of dots on the top end of the domino is the numerator, and the number of dots on the bottom is the denominator.

2. Turn the domino over to find the fraction. Is the fraction proper or improper? If the numerator is smaller than the denominator, as in 3/5, 2/3, and 1/6, then the fraction is proper, or less than 1. If the numerator is greater than or equal to the denominator, as in 5/3, 6/4, 5/2, 3/1, and 3/3, then the fraction is improper or greater than 1.

3. If you guessed correctly, place the domino on the piece of paper marked Correct. If you guessed incorrectly, place the domino on the piece of paper marked Incorrect.

4. Continue down the row, guessing whether the fraction represented on each domino is proper or improper.

5. Are you psychic? How many fractions did you guess correctly, and how many did you guess incorrectly?

SUPER DOMINO ESP

Play the game again, this time guessing whether each domino represents a proper fraction, an improper fraction, or a whole number. With three categories, your chances of guessing correctly are even less. Here are some examples of fractions that are equivalent to whole numbers:

- If the numerator is equal to the denominator, as in 1/1, 2/2, 3/3, 4/4, 5/5, and 6/6, then the fraction is equivalent to 1, a whole number.

- If the denominator is 1, as in 1/1, 2/1, 3/1, 4/1, 5/1, and 6/1, then the fraction is equivalent to a whole number as indicated by the numerator. So 1/1 = 1, 2/1 = 2, 3/1 = 3, and so on.

- If the numerator is a multiple of the denominator, as in 9/3, 4/2, and 6/2, then the fraction is equivalent to a whole number. Divide the numerator by the denominator to get the whole number. For example, 9 ÷ 3 = 3, 4 ÷ 2 = 2, and 6 ÷ 2 = 3.

Flip It!

A "mixed number" is a whole number plus a fraction. Play this game to practice changing improper fractions to mixed numbers.

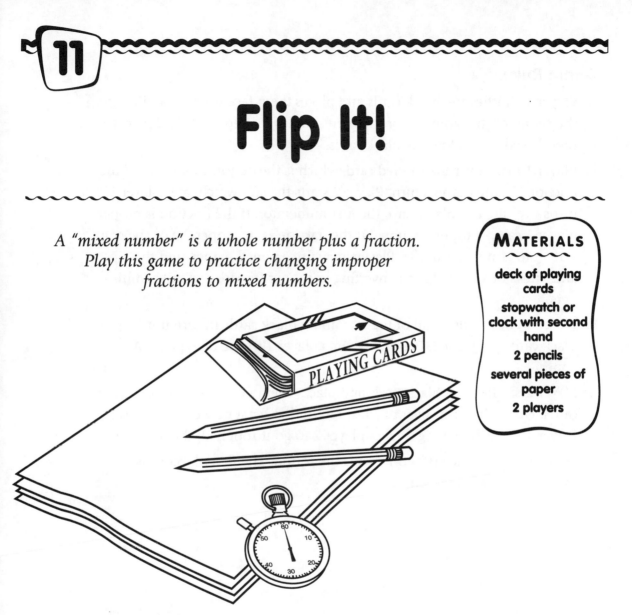

Game Preparation

1. Remove all the face cards (kings, queens, and jacks) from a deck of playing cards.

2. Sort the playing cards into a stack of black cards and a stack of red cards based on color of suit. These two stacks will be used to construct fractions. The black cards are the numerators and the red cards are the denominators. Aces count as 1's.

Game Rules

1. Player 1 shuffles the black cards and places them facedown in a pile in the center of the table. He or she then shuffles the red cards and places them facedown below the black cards.

2. Player 1 turns over the top red card, which is the denominator for all the fractions in the player's turn. Player 2 starts the stopwatch, and player 1 turns over the top black card, the first numerator. If the fraction is proper, player 1 says, "Proper fraction." If the fraction is improper, he or she converts it to a mixed number. Players may use a pencil, paper, and the Tips and Tricks box for help in converting improper fractions to mixed numbers.

3. Player 1 goes through all of the remaining black cards in turn until all the black cards are played. Player 2 records player 1's time on a piece of paper.

4. Player 2 shuffles the black cards and places them facedown above the red cards. He or she turns over the next red card to get a new denominator. Player 1 times how long it takes player 2 to go through all the black cards.

5. The player with the faster time wins the round. The first player to win three rounds wins the game.

Tips and Tricks

To convert an improper fraction to a mixed number, follow these two simple steps:

1. Divide the numerator by the denominator. The quotient will be a whole number with a "remainder," a number left over when two numbers cannot be evenly divided. The remainder is abbreviated "R." For example, if the improper fraction is $\frac{8}{3}$, then $8 \div 3 = 2$ R2.

2. To write the quotient as a mixed number, put the whole number first and then make the fraction using the remainder as the numerator over the original denominator. So $\frac{8}{3}$ becomes $2\frac{2}{3}$.

SUPER FLIP IT!

Play Super Flip It! the same way you play Flip It! except rather than say, "Proper fraction," reduce all proper fractions to their lowest terms and call out the lowest-terms fraction.

Cut Up!

Now that you know how to change improper fractions to mixed numbers, practice changing mixed numbers to improper fractions.

MATERIALS

paper plates
scissors
pencil
paper

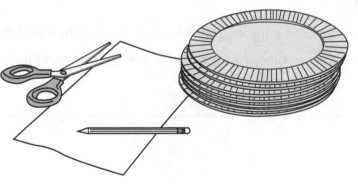

Procedure

1. Use paper plates to change a mixed number to an improper fraction. For example, to convert $1\frac{3}{4}$ to an improper fraction:

   a. Take two paper plates and cut one of them into four equal parts. Put one of the four small pieces aside and keep three. You have one and three-quarters $\left(1\frac{3}{4}\right)$ plates.

   b. Cut the other plate into four equal parts. Count how many fourths you have altogether: 4 + 3 = 7. You have seven-fourths $\left(\frac{7}{4}\right)$, so the mixed number $1\frac{3}{4}$ equals the improper fraction $\frac{7}{4}$.

2. To convert $4\frac{1}{2}$ to an improper fraction:

   a. Take five plates. Cut one paper plate in half and discard one half. You have four and a half $\left(4\frac{1}{2}\right)$ plates.

b. Cut the other four plates in half. Count how many halves you have altogether: 8 + 1 = 9. You have nine halves $\left(\frac{9}{2}\right)$, so $4\frac{1}{2} = \frac{9}{2}$.

3. Use this method to convert the following mixed numbers to improper fractions. Or, instead of paper plates, you can use a pencil, paper, and the Tips and Tricks box for help.

$6\frac{2}{3}$

$7\frac{1}{2}$

$8\frac{1}{3}$

$6\frac{2}{5}$

$7\frac{1}{4}$

Tips and Tricks

To convert a mixed number to an improper fraction without using plates, follow these two simple steps. The mixed number in the example is $2\frac{1}{5}$.

1. Multiply the denominator of the fraction by the whole number: $5 \times 2 = 10$.

2. Add the product to the numerator: $10 + 1 = 11$. The "sum" (addition answer) becomes the numerator of the improper fraction. So the mixed number $2\frac{1}{5}$ is equivalent to the improper fraction $\frac{11}{5}$.

   Here is how the problem is written:

   $2\frac{1}{5} = \frac{(5 \times 2) + 1}{5} = \frac{10 + 1}{5} = \frac{11}{5}$

The parentheses around the numbers mean that these numbers are multiplied first, then the product is added to the number following the plus sign. The sum is the numerator of the improper fraction.

Zero

Play Zero to learn what to do when 0 is in a fraction.

Game Preparation

Copy one of the following fractions on each of 14 index cards:

| 0/1 | 0/5 | 0/10 | 0/50 | 0/100 | 0/500 | 0/1,000 |
| 1/0 | 5/0 | 10/0 | 50/0 | 100/0 | 500/0 | 1,000/0 |

Game Rules

1. Shuffle the cards.

2. Player 2 starts a stopwatch and holds up one of the cards for player 1 to see. If the value of the fraction on the card is 0, player 1 holds up his or her thumb and forefinger to make the shape of a 0. If the value of the fraction is undefined, player 1 makes a thumbs-down motion. Players can use the Tips and Tricks box for help in remembering the difference between these types of fractions.

3. Player 2 stops the stopwatch when player 1 correctly identifies the fractions on all 14 cards as having a value of 0 or undefined. The player who makes it through the whole deck of cards faster is the winner.

Tips and Tricks

Zero can be either the numerator or the denominator of a fraction. If 0 is the numerator, the fraction is equal to 0.

0/5 = 0

0/12 = 0

0/1,000 = 0

If 0 is the denominator, the fraction is undefined. Nothing can be divided into zero parts.

3/0 is undefined.

7/0 is undefined.

1/0 is undefined.

No matter what the numerator is, if the denominator is 0 the fraction is always undefined.

III

ADDING AND SUBTRACTING FRACTIONS

Now that you know fraction basics, it is time to learn how to add and subtract fractions. You'll learn how to add and subtract fractions that have common denominators and fractions that have different denominators. You'll add mixed numbers to mixed numbers, mixed numbers to proper fractions, and fractions to whole numbers. You'll subtract all kinds of fractions, too.

Along the way, you will make paper pizzas, trade poker chips, make pattern pictures, play tic-tac-toe, roll fraction dice, create fractions with dominoes, and play lots of different games.

14

Combination Pizza

Make an ultimate combination of pizza slices that add up to one pie while you learn how to add fractions with common denominators.

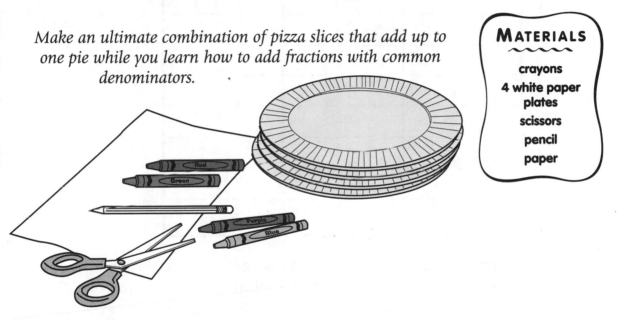

MATERIALS

crayons

4 white paper plates

scissors

pencil

paper

Procedure

1. Use your crayons and four paper plates to design four different pizzas: a pepperoni pizza, a green pepper pizza, a pineapple pizza, and a plain cheese pizza.

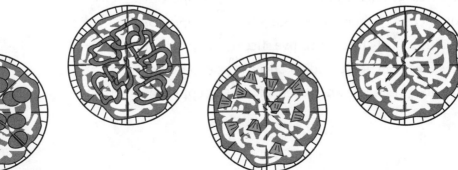

2. Cut each pizza into eight equal slices.

3. Copy the Pizza Fractions table on a piece of paper.

PIZZA FRACTIONS

Number of Slices	Fraction	Reduced Fraction
1	$\frac{1}{8}$	$\frac{1}{8}$
2	$\frac{2}{8}$	$\frac{1}{4}$
3	$\frac{3}{8}$	$\frac{3}{8}$
4	$\frac{4}{8}$	$\frac{1}{2}$
5	$\frac{5}{8}$	$\frac{5}{8}$
6	$\frac{6}{8}$	$\frac{3}{4}$
7	$\frac{7}{8}$	$\frac{7}{8}$
8	$\frac{8}{8}$	$\frac{1}{1}$, or 1

4. How many ways can you make a whole pizza using slices from two different pizzas? Use your paper pizzas to make a whole pizza that is a combination of, say, cheese slices and pepperoni slices. There are seven ways to make a whole pizza that is a combination of cheese and pepperoni:

seven slices $\left(\frac{7}{8}\right)$ cheese and one slice $\left(\frac{1}{8}\right)$ pepperoni

six slices $\left(\frac{3}{4}\right)$ cheese and two slices $\left(\frac{1}{4}\right)$ pepperoni

five slices $\left(\frac{5}{8}\right)$ cheese and three slices $\left(\frac{3}{8}\right)$ pepperoni

four slices $\left(\frac{1}{2}\right)$ cheese and four slices $\left(\frac{1}{2}\right)$ pepperoni

three slices $\left(\frac{1}{8}\right)$ cheese and five slices $\left(\frac{5}{8}\right)$ pepperoni

two slices $\left(\frac{1}{4}\right)$ cheese and six slices $\left(\frac{3}{4}\right)$ pepperoni

one slice $\left(\frac{1}{8}\right)$ cheese and seven slices $\left(\frac{7}{8}\right)$ pepperoni

5. By making these pizzas, you've started adding fractions that have common denominators. When adding fractions that have common denominators, the denominator stays the same while the numerators are added. The following problems show how to add the cheese and pepperoni slices to make one combination pizza:

$$\frac{7}{8} + \frac{1}{8} = \frac{7+1}{8} = \frac{8}{8} = 1$$

$$\frac{3}{4} + \frac{1}{4} = \frac{3+1}{4} = \frac{4}{4} = 1$$

$$\frac{5}{8} + \frac{3}{8} = \frac{5+3}{8} = \frac{8}{8} = 1$$

$$\frac{1}{2} + \frac{1}{2} = \frac{1+1}{2} = \frac{2}{2} = 1$$

$$\frac{3}{8} + \frac{5}{8} = \frac{3+5}{8} = \frac{8}{8} = 1$$

$$\frac{1}{4} + \frac{3}{4} = \frac{1+3}{4} = \frac{4}{4} = 1$$

$$\frac{1}{8} + \frac{7}{8} = \frac{1+7}{8} = \frac{8}{8} = 1$$

6. How many ways can you make a whole pizza using three different pizzas? How about four different pizzas? Use your paper pizzas to find out.

15

Addition Chip Trading

*Use poker chips to practice adding mixed numbers
that have common denominators.*

MATERIALS

poker chips (red
and white, or any
other two colors)
or nickels and
pennies

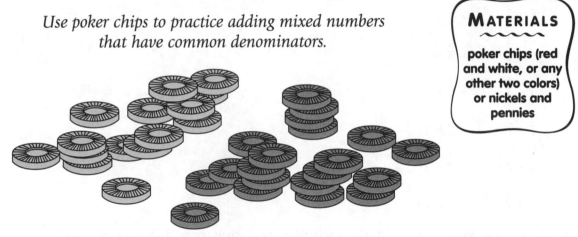

Procedure

1. Use red chips or nickels to represent the whole number of a mixed number and white chips or pennies to represent the numerator of the fraction. For example, the mixed number $6\frac{3}{4}$ is represented by six red chips or nickels and three white chips or pennies. The denominator is 4, meaning four parts make a whole, so four white chips are equal to one red chip.

2. To add two mixed numbers that have same-color common denominators:

   a. Start by grouping like chips. For example, to add $6\frac{3}{4}$ and $2\frac{3}{4}$, first add the whole numbers: 6 + 2 = 8. Make a group of eight red chips for the whole numbers. Then add the numerators: 3 + 3 = 6. Make a group of six white chips for the numerators.

   b. Trade in your white chips for red chips. Since the common denominator is 4, for every four white chips you'll get one red chip. You have six white chips, so when you trade in four of them, you'll get one red chip and still have two white chips. These traded chips represent the mixed number $1\frac{2}{4}$.

c. Add the traded chips to the group of eight red chips: $1\frac{2}{4} + 8 = 9\frac{2}{4}$.

d. Reduce the fraction from $9\frac{2}{4}$ to $9\frac{1}{2}$. So $6\frac{3}{4} + 2\frac{3}{4} = 8\frac{6}{4} = 9\frac{2}{4} = 9\frac{1}{2}$.

3. Use chip trading to solve the following problems:

$6\frac{1}{4} + 2\frac{1}{4}$

$5\frac{3}{4} + 4\frac{1}{4}$

4. Now use chip trading and the Tips and Tricks box to solve these problems. Since 8 is the common denominator, trade eight white chips for one red chip.

$4\frac{3}{8} + 5\frac{1}{8}$

$6\frac{1}{8} + 1\frac{5}{8}$

$4\frac{5}{8} + \frac{5}{8}$

$3\frac{7}{8} + 6\frac{3}{8}$

Tips and Tricks

To add two mixed numbers that have common denominators, follow these four simple steps. The problem in this example is $3\frac{3}{5} + 4\frac{4}{5}$.

1. Add the whole numbers: $3 + 4 = 7$.

2. Add the fractions by adding the numerators: $\frac{3}{5} + \frac{4}{5} = \frac{7}{5}$.

3. If the resulting fraction is improper, convert it to a whole or mixed number by dividing the numerator by the denominator. The remainder, if any, becomes a numerator: $\frac{7}{5} = 1\frac{2}{5}$.

4. Add the mixed number to the sum of the whole numbers:

$1\frac{2}{5} + 7 = 8\frac{2}{5}$. So $3\frac{3}{5} + 4\frac{4}{5} = 7\frac{7}{5} = 8\frac{2}{5}$.

Try adding four or five mixed numbers using chip trading. Just make sure all the numbers have the same common denominator.

1. What is $6\frac{7}{12} + 7\frac{5}{12} + 1\frac{1}{12} + 4\frac{11}{12}$?

For $6\frac{7}{12}$ use six red chips and seven white chips.

For $7\frac{5}{12}$ use seven red chips and five white chips.

For $1\frac{1}{12}$ use one red chip and one white chip.

For $4\frac{11}{12}$ use four red chips and eleven white chips.

Group all the red chips together to get $6 + 7 + 1 + 4 = 18$ red chips. Group all the white chips together to get $7 + 5 + 1 + 11 = 24$ white chips.

Since 12 is the common denominator, you can trade 12 white chips for one red chip. This gives you two more red chips and no white chips remaining. Add these to the group of 18 red chips to make 20 red chips. The answer is 20.

2. What is $5\frac{1}{9} + 6\frac{2}{9} + 4\frac{7}{9} + 13\frac{3}{9} + 1\frac{8}{9}$?

16

Pattern Pictures

*Practice subtracting fractions that
have common denominators.*

MATERIALS

pencil

**several pieces of
paper**

**graph paper
(large grid)**

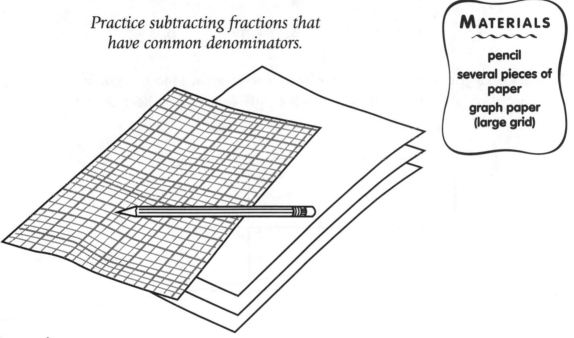

Procedure

1. To subtract fractions that have common denominators, first subtract the
numerators to find the "difference" (subtraction answer). Place the difference over the denominator. Then reduce the fraction if necessary.

For example, what is $\frac{3}{5} - \frac{1}{5}$?

Subtract the numerators: $3 - 1 = 2$.

Place the difference over the denominator: $\frac{2}{5}$.

Reduce: It's impossible to reduce $\frac{2}{5}$.

2. Solve the following problems. Reduce the fractions to their lowest terms. Write the answers on a separate piece of paper and label them from *a* to *p*.

a. $\frac{3}{5} - \frac{1}{5}$

b. $\frac{4}{4} - \frac{1}{4}$

c. $\frac{5}{10} - \frac{1}{10}$

d. $\frac{7}{16} - \frac{4}{16}$

e. $\frac{10}{11} - \frac{9}{11}$

f. $\frac{2}{3} - \frac{1}{3}$

g. $\frac{6}{7} - \frac{5}{7}$

h. $\frac{4}{5} - \frac{3}{5}$

i. $\frac{7}{12} - \frac{2}{12}$

j. $\frac{5}{6} - \frac{3}{6}$

k. $\frac{3}{8} - \frac{1}{8}$

l. $\frac{6}{7} - \frac{2}{7}$

m. $\frac{19}{25} - \frac{13}{25}$

n. $\frac{7}{9} - \frac{2}{9}$

o. $\frac{7}{11} - \frac{3}{11}$

p. $\frac{6}{7} - \frac{0}{7}$

3. Mark off a grid that is four squares by four squares on a piece of graph paper. Write the letters from *a* to *p* in the squares as shown. Keep the letters small.

a	b	c	d
e	f	g	h
i	j	k	l
m	n	o	p

4. The letters in the squares of the grid correspond to the letters of the answers to the problems. To fill in the squares of the grid, look at the numerator of each answer. If the numerator is 1, shade the entire box. If the numerator is 2, 3, 4, or 5, shade half of the box in one of the ways indicated on the next page. If the numerator is 6, leave the box empty. Your shading will create a sweet design.

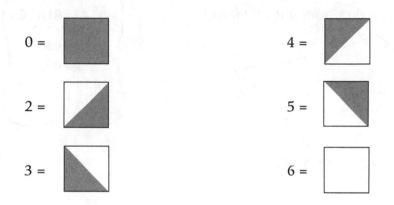

0 =

2 =

3 =

4 =

5 =

6 =

17

Circles inside Circles

Practice subtracting a fraction from a whole number.

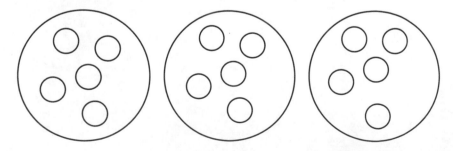

Procedure

1. Look at the problem $3 - \frac{3}{5}$. Draw three circles to represent the whole number.

2. Look at the denominator of the number you are subtracting: 5. Draw five little circles inside each large circle, as shown. Now each circle represents $\frac{5}{5}$, which is equal to 1.

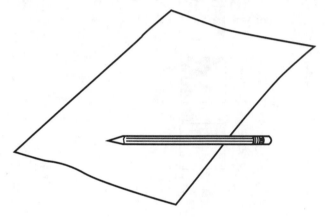

3. Look at the numerator of the number you are subtracting: 3. Erase three small circles from the third circle.

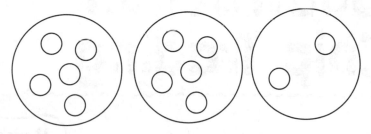

4. Two small circles are left in the third circle. You have two whole circles and two-fifths $\left(\frac{2}{5}\right)$ of the last circle, so $3 - \frac{3}{5} = 2\frac{2}{5}$.

5. Use the circle method and the method in the Tips and Tricks box to solve the following problems:

$$7 - \frac{1}{4}$$

$$10 - \frac{4}{7}$$

$$14 - \frac{3}{8}$$

Tips and Tricks

To subtract a fraction from a whole number, follow these three simple steps. The problem in this example is $6 - \frac{2}{3}$.

1. Reduce the whole number by 1 and convert the 1 you took away into a fraction that has the same numerator and denominator as the denominator of the fraction you are subtracting. So 6 becomes $5\frac{3}{3}$.

2. Subtract the fraction in the problem from $\left(\frac{2}{3}\right)$ from the converted fraction using the method in chapter 16 for subtracting fractions with common denominators: $5\frac{3}{3} - \frac{2}{3} = 5\frac{1}{3}$.

3. Reduce the fraction if necessary: $5\frac{1}{3}$ cannot be reduced. So $6 - \frac{2}{3} = 5\frac{1}{3}$.

18

Subtraction Chip Trading

Practice subtracting mixed numbers that have common denominators.

MATERIALS

poker chips (yellow and blue, or any other two colors) or nickels and pennies

pencil

paper

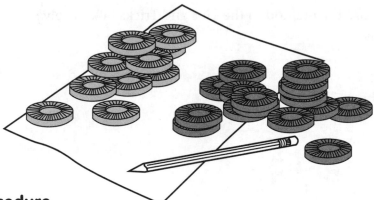

Procedure

1. To subtract mixed numbers that have common denominators, first change the "minuend" (the number you are subtracting from) to chips or coins. Use yellow chips or nickels to represent the whole number and blue chips or pennies to represent the numerator of the fraction. For example, in the problem $4\frac{3}{5} - 1\frac{4}{5}$, the mixed number $4\frac{3}{5}$ is represented by four yellow chips or nickels and three blue chips or pennies. The common denominator is 5, so five blue chips are equal to one yellow chip.

2. To subtract $1\frac{4}{5}$ from $4\frac{3}{5}$, take away one yellow chip and four blue chips. Since you don't have four blue chips, trade one yellow chip for five blue chips. This gives you three yellow chips and eight blue chips (or $3\frac{8}{5}$). Now you can take away one yellow chip and four blue chips. There are two yellow chips and four blue chips remaining. So $4\frac{3}{5} - 1\frac{4}{5} = 3\frac{8}{5} - 1\frac{4}{5} = 2\frac{4}{5}$.

3. Use chip trading to solve the following problems. Or instead you can use a pencil, paper, and the Tips and Tricks box for help in subtracting mixed numbers.

$$6\tfrac{1}{4} - 3\tfrac{1}{4}$$

$$5\tfrac{2}{3} - 2\tfrac{1}{3}$$

$$6\tfrac{3}{8} - 1\tfrac{5}{8}$$

Tips and Tricks

To subtract mixed numbers that have common denominators, follow these two simple steps:

1. Subtract the numerators. If the numerator of the minuend is smaller than that of the "subtrahend" (the number you are subtracting), subtract 1 from the whole number of the minuend and carry the numerator to the fraction. For example, in the problem $7\tfrac{1}{5} - 6\tfrac{4}{5}$, $\tfrac{1}{5}$ is smaller than $\tfrac{4}{5}$. Subtract 1 from 7, change this 1 to $\tfrac{5}{5}$, and add this to the fraction. So the minuend $7\tfrac{1}{5}$ becomes $6\tfrac{6}{5}$, and the problem becomes $6\tfrac{6}{5} - 6\tfrac{4}{5}$. Now you can subtract the numerators: $\tfrac{6}{5} - \tfrac{4}{5} = \tfrac{2}{5}$.

2. Subtract the whole numbers: $6 - 6 = 0$. So $7\tfrac{1}{5} - 6\tfrac{4}{5} = \tfrac{2}{5}$.

   Sometimes subtracting the numerators gives you a fraction that is not in its lowest terms. For example, in the problem $3\tfrac{3}{4} - 2\tfrac{1}{4}$, subtracting $\tfrac{1}{4}$ from $\tfrac{3}{4}$ gives you $\tfrac{2}{4}$. Reduce the fraction, so $\tfrac{2}{4}$ becomes $\tfrac{1}{2}$. Now subtract the whole numbers: $3 - 2 = 1$. So $3\tfrac{3}{4} - 2\tfrac{1}{4} = 1\tfrac{1}{2}$.

19 Least Common Multiple Tic-Tac-Toe

To add or subtract fractions that don't have common denominators, you have to first find the least common multiple of the denominators. Practice finding the least common multiple while playing tic-tac-toe.

MATERIALS

playing cards

2 pencils

several pieces of paper

stopwatch or clock with second hand

2 players

Game Preparation

1. Remove all the aces and face cards (kings, queens, and jacks) from a deck of playing cards.

2. Draw a tic-tac-toe board on a piece of paper.

Game Rules

1. Shuffle the cards and place them facedown on the table.

2. Player 1 turns over the top two cards and places them side by side. Player 1 has 15 seconds to find the least common multiple of these numbers. If correct, he or she places an **X** on the tic-tac-toe board. If incorrect, it is player 2's turn. Players can use a pencil, paper, and the Tips and Tricks and Advanced Tips and Tricks boxes for help in determining the least common multiple.

3. Player 2 turns over the next two cards. He or she now has 15 seconds to find the correct least common multiple and place an **O** on the tic-tac-toe board.

4. The game continues until one player wins by getting three **X**'s or **O**'s in a row or neither player gets three in a row and all the squares are filled.

Tips and Tricks

To find the least common multiple of two numbers, follow these three simple steps. The numbers in this example are 6 and 10.

1. List the first 10 multiples of each number.
   a. The first 10 multiples of 6 are 6, 12, 18, 24, 30, 36, 42, 48, 54, and 60.
   b. The first 10 multiples of 10 are 10, 20, 30, 40, 50, 60, 70, 80, 90, and 100.
2. Circle the multiples the two numbers have in common: 30 and 60.
3. Put a square around the smallest multiple the two numbers have in common: 30. This is the least common multiple. And it is also the lowest common denominator when two fractions have different denominators—in this case, 6 and 10.

Tips and Tricks

Here's a trick that will save you some time. If both numbers are "prime" (divisible only by themselves and 1), simply multiply them to get the least common multiple!

What's the least common multiple of 5 and 7? First try the long way:

The first 10 multiples of 5 are 5, 10, 15, 20, 25, 30, 35, 40, 45, and 50.

The first 10 multiples of 7 are 7, 14, 21, 28, 35, 42, 49, 56, 63, and 70.

The only multiple (so far) these two numbers have in common is 35, which is the product of 5×7. So 35 is the least common multiple of 5 and 7 because they are both prime numbers.

Quick Change

To add or subtract fractions that don't have a common denominator, you need to change one or both to equivalent fractions that do have a common denominator. Here's a game that will give you practice creating equivalent fractions.

MATERIALS

playing cards
pencil
index cards
2 or more players

Game Preparation

1. Remove all the face cards (kings, queens, and jacks) from a deck of playing cards.

2. Write one of the following fractions on each of 20 index cards.

1/2	3/4	4/5	4/7	3/8
1/3	1/5	1/6	5/7	5/8
2/3	2/5	1/7	6/7	7/8
1/4	3/5	3/7	1/8	1/10

Game Rules

1. Shuffle the playing cards and place them facedown in a stack on the table. Shuffle the fraction cards and place them facedown beside the playing cards.

2. Turn over the top fraction card and place it faceup.

3. Players take turns drawing the top card from the deck of playing cards and multiplying both the numerator and the denominator on the fraction card by the number on the playing card. The fraction created is equivalent to the original fraction. Say the fraction card is 4/5 and the playing card is the 3 of clubs. First multiply the numerator by 3 to create a new numerator: $4 \times 3 = 12$. Then multiply the denominator by 3 to create a new denominator: $5 \times 3 = 15$. The created fraction is 12/15, and it is equivalent to 4/5.

4. If a player makes a mistake, he or she "wins" the fraction card. If neither player makes a mistake through the entire stack of playing cards, a new fraction card is turned over, the playing cards are shuffled and placed facedown on the table, and another round is played.

5. The first player to "win" three cards loses the game.

BRAIN Stretchers

You can change any fraction to an equivalent fraction by multiplying the numerator and the denominator of the fraction by the same number.

1. Convert the fraction 1/2 to an equivalent fraction. Multiply the numerator and the denominator of 1/2 by

    2 and the result is 2/4.

    3 and the result is 3/6.

    4 and the result is 4/8.

2. Convert the fraction 3/4 to an equivalent fraction. Multiply the numerator and the denominator of 3/4 by

    2 and the result is 6/8.

    3 and the result is 9/12.

    4 and the result is 12/16.

3. In order to find a common denominator, you have to find a specific equivalent fraction. Convert the fraction 2/3 to a fraction with the denominator 15. What number do you have to multiply the denominator by to get 15? To find out, divide 15 by 3 to get 5. Since you multiply the denominator by 5, you must multiply the numerator by 5 also. If you multiply both the numerator and the denominator of 2/3 by 5, the equivalent fraction is 10/15. This will come in handy if you need to add 2/3 to a fraction like 4/15.

Fraction Roll

Now that you know how to create equivalent fractions that have common denominators, play this game to practice adding two fractions that have different denominators.

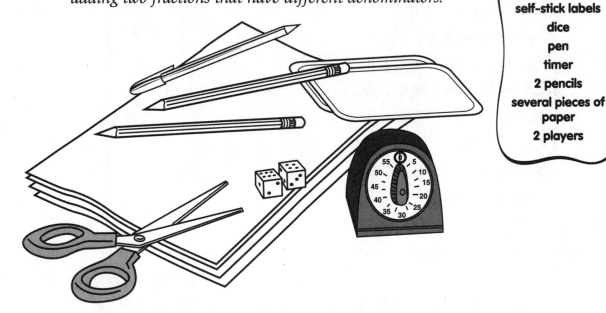

Game Preparation

1. Cut self-stick labels into 12 small squares that are the same size as the face of a die.

2. Write each of the following fractions on its own small square:

$$\frac{1}{6} \qquad \frac{1}{4} \qquad \frac{1}{3} \qquad \frac{1}{2} \qquad \frac{2}{3} \qquad \frac{3}{4}$$

3. Stick each of the small squares on a different face of one die.

4. Repeat steps 1 to 3 to cover the second die with fractions. These are your fraction dice.

Game Rules

1. Player 1 rolls the fraction dice and player 2 sets the timer. Player 1 has 20 seconds to add the fractions on the dice and reduce the answer to its lowest terms. Players can use a pencil, paper, and the Tips and Tricks box for help in adding and reducing fractions. If player 1 is correct, he or she earns 1 point. If the two fractions rolled add up to exactly 1, the player earns 2 points.

2. Player 2 rolls the dice and adds the fractions on them while player 1 serves as timekeeper.

3. The first player to earn 10 points wins the game.

SUPER FRACTION ROLL

Make a third fraction die. Roll all three dice and add the fractions. Players have 30 seconds to get the correct answer.

Tips and Tricks

To add fractions that have different denominators and reduce them to lowest terms, follow these four simple steps. The fractions in this example are $\frac{5}{8}$ and $\frac{1}{2}$.

1. Find the common denominator by finding the least common multiple.

   The multiples of 2 are 2, 4, 6, 8, 10, 12, 14, 16, 18, 20, and so on.

   The multiples of 8 are 8, 16, 24, 32, 40, 48, 56, 64, 72, 80, and so on.

   The common multiple of 2 and 8 is 8, so 8 is the least common denominator.

2. Convert each fraction to an equivalent fraction using the common denominator. The common denominator is 8, so divide 8 by the denominator of the original fraction, $\frac{1}{2}$: $8 \div 2 = 4$. Multiply the quotient by the original numerator to get the new numerator: $4 \times 1 = 4$. So $\frac{1}{2}$ becomes the equivalent fraction $\frac{4}{8}$. (Since the denominator of $\frac{5}{8}$ is 8, you don't have to convert $\frac{5}{8}$.)

3. Add the two equivalent fractions by adding their numerators: $\frac{4}{8} + \frac{5}{8} = \frac{9}{8}$.

4. If the fraction is improper, convert it to a mixed number and reduce the fraction if necessary. Since $\frac{9}{8}$ is an improper fraction, convert it to a mixed number by subtracting $\frac{8}{8}$: $\frac{9}{8} - \frac{8}{8} = \frac{1}{8}$. The $\frac{8}{8}$ you subtracted becomes the whole number 1 in the mixed number $1\frac{1}{8}$. So $\frac{4}{8} + \frac{5}{8} = 1\frac{1}{8}$.

22

Up-and-Down Dominoes

Practice adding proper and improper fractions.

Game Preparation

1. Remove all the dominoes that are blank on one or both ends.

2. Give each player a pencil and a piece of paper.

Game Rules

1. Mix the remaining dominoes and spread them out facedown on the table.

2. Each player picks a domino at random and turns it faceup. Each player uses his or her domino to make two fractions. The dots on one end of the domino are the numerator and the dots on the other end are the denominator of one fraction. Turn the domino upside down to make the other fraction. For example, if the domino has two dots one end and three dots on the other end, the first fraction is $\frac{2}{3}$ (a proper fraction) and the second fraction is $\frac{3}{2}$ (an improper fraction). Each player writes his or her fractions on a piece of paper.

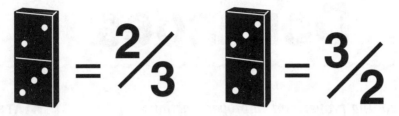

3. Each player adds the two fractions as fast as he or she can. For the fractions $\frac{2}{3}$ and $\frac{3}{2}$, the least common multiple of 3 and 2 is 6. Convert both fractions to sixths: $\frac{2}{3} = \frac{4}{6}$, and $\frac{3}{2} = \frac{9}{6}$. Now add the fractions: $\frac{4}{6} + \frac{9}{6} = \frac{13}{6}$. Convert $\frac{13}{6}$ to a mixed number by dividing 6 into 13: $\frac{13}{6} = 2\frac{1}{6}$.

4. The first player to correctly add his or her fractions wins the round. The first player to win three rounds wins the game.

SUPER UP-AND-DOWN DOMINOES

Each player picks up two dominoes and adds all four of the fractions created.

UP-AND-DOWN DOMINOES SOLITAIRE

You can play the game alone as well. Just get a stopwatch and time yourself as you solve the problems. Try to improve your speed each time you play.

23

Missing Numbers

Practice subtracting mixed numbers while you
solve missing-number problems.

MATERIALS

pencil
paper

Procedure

1. All three of these problems are missing the same number. The letter x stands for the missing number. Can you figure out what it is?

$$7\frac{4}{x} - 2\frac{1}{5} = x\frac{3}{5}$$

Hint: One easy way to solve for x is to add the difference to the subtrahend. Remember, when adding mixed numbers, add the fractions first, then the whole numbers. Remember also that the difference can be a reduced fraction, so the subtrahend or the minuend may have a different denominator. When you think you've found the missing number, substitute it for x and work the subtraction problem to see if you're correct.

2. These two problems have the same missing number. What is it?

$$x\frac{1}{x} - 2\frac{1}{6} = 1\frac{1}{6}$$

$$x\frac{1}{x} - x\frac{1}{6} = \frac{1}{2}$$

BRAIN Stretcher

Create a group of three missing-number problems. Give them to a friend or family member to solve. In each group of problems, let a number from 1 to 9 be the missing number for every problem—the same missing number for all problems in the group. Make three different groups of problems for your friend to solve.

~~~ IV ~~~
MULTIPLYING AND DIVIDING FRACTIONS

Now that you know how to add and subtract fractions, it is time to learn how to multiply and divide fractions. You'll learn how to multiply and divide fractions and fractions, fractions and whole numbers, fractions and mixed numbers, and mixed numbers and mixed  numbers. There are lots of different types of multiplication and division problems, but once you get the basic idea they are all the same.

In this section, you'll go on an imaginary shopping spree, split a deck of cards in various ways, do fraction problems with dominoes, create magic fraction squares, play a game with the lid of a shoe box, and have fun in many other ways.

24

Graph Paper Multiplication

Practice multiplying two fractions using graph paper and colored pencils.

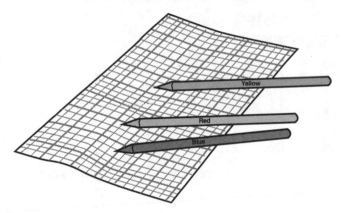

Procedure

1. Use graph paper and colored pencils or crayons to solve the problem $\frac{1}{4} \times \frac{2}{3}$.

   a. Look at the denominators of the fractions you are multiplying. The denominators of the fractions $\frac{1}{4}$ and $\frac{2}{3}$ are 4 and 3.

   b. On the graph paper, draw a rectangle whose sides are the "lengths" of the denominators. So for $\frac{1}{4}$ and $\frac{2}{3}$, draw a rectangle that is four squares long (columns) and three squares high (rows). There are 12 squares altogether.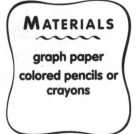

c. Color one of the columns to represent the fraction $\frac{1}{4}$, or one-fourth of the rectangle.

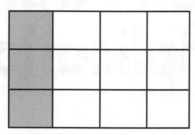

d. Using a different colored pencil, color two of the rows to represent the fraction $\frac{2}{3}$, or two-thirds of the rectangle. You will need to color over two of the squares colored in step 1c.

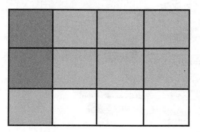

e. Count the number of squares that are colored twice. Two squares are colored twice.

f. Divide the number of squares colored twice by 12, the total number of squares. The answer is $\frac{2}{12}$. Reduce the fraction from $\frac{2}{12}$ to $\frac{1}{6}$.
So $\frac{1}{4} \times \frac{2}{3} = \frac{1}{6}$.

2. Use graph paper and colored pencils to solve the problem $\frac{3}{8} \times \frac{5}{6}$.

a. Look at the denominators of the fractions $\frac{3}{8}$ and $\frac{5}{6}$. The denominators are 8 and 6.

b. Draw a rectangle that is eight squares long and six squares high. There are 48 squares altogether.

c. Color five of the six rows to represent $\frac{5}{6}$. You've shaded five-sixths of the rectangle.

d. Color three of eight columns to represent $\frac{3}{8}$, coloring over some of the squares in step 2c. You've now colored three-eighths of the rectangle.

e. Count the number of squares that are colored twice: 15.

f. Divide the number of squares colored twice by 48, the total number of squares. The answer is $\frac{15}{48}$. So $\frac{3}{8} \times \frac{5}{6} = \frac{15}{48}$. Reduce the fraction from $\frac{15}{48}$ to $\frac{5}{16}$.

3. You can use graph paper and colored pencils to multiply any two fractions. Try to solve these problems:

$$\frac{1}{2} \times \frac{1}{2}$$

$$\frac{3}{4} \times \frac{1}{3}$$

$$\frac{2}{3} \times \frac{1}{2}$$

$$\frac{1}{6} \times \frac{2}{5}$$

$$\frac{1}{10} \times \frac{3}{10}$$

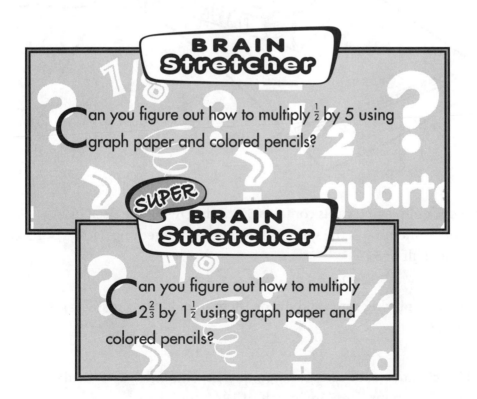

BRAIN Stretcher

Can you figure out how to multiply $\frac{1}{2}$ by 5 using graph paper and colored pencils?

SUPER BRAIN Stretcher

Can you figure out how to multiply $2\frac{2}{3}$ by $1\frac{1}{2}$ using graph paper and colored pencils?

MATERIALS

deck of playing cards

pencil

paper

25

Splitting the Deck

Divide a deck of cards in different ways to learn how to multiply a fraction by a whole number.

Procedure

1. A standard deck of playing cards contains 52 cards. Divide the deck in half. "Half of" something is the same as saying "$\frac{1}{2} \times$" something. How many cards are half of 52?

$$\frac{1}{2} \times 52 = \frac{1}{2} \times \frac{52}{1} = \frac{1 \times 52}{2 \times 1} = \frac{52}{2} = 26$$

2. Take the 26 black playing cards and divide them in half. How many cards are in half of 26?

$$\frac{1}{2} \times 26 = \frac{1}{2} \times \frac{26}{1} = \frac{1 \times 26}{2 \times 1} = \frac{26}{2} = 13$$

3. Take the 12 face cards (four each of kings, queens, and jacks) and divide them in half. How many cards are in half of 12?

$$\frac{1}{2} \times 12 = \frac{1}{2} \times \frac{12}{1} = \frac{1 \times 12}{2 \times 1} = \frac{12}{2} = 6$$

4. Take the four aces and four kings, which is a total of eight cards; then take three-fourths of them. (Make four equal piles and take three of them. Count the number of cards in these three piles.) How many cards are in three-fourths of eight?

$$\frac{3}{4} \times 8 = \frac{3}{4} \times \frac{8}{1} = \frac{3 \times 8}{4 \times 1} = \frac{24}{4} = 6$$

5. Take the 12 face cards again; then take two-thirds of them. (Make three equal piles and take two of them. Count the number of cards in these two piles.) How many cards are in two-thirds of 12?

$$\frac{2}{3} \times 12 = \frac{2}{3} \times \frac{12}{1} = \frac{2 \times 12}{3 \times 1} = \frac{24}{3} = 8$$

6. Make up your own fraction problems, using a pencil, paper, and the Tips and Tricks box for help. Then solve your problems.

Tips and Tricks

To multiply a fraction by a whole number, follow these two simple steps. The problem in this example is $\frac{3}{4} \times 20$.

1. Convert the whole number to a fraction: 20 becomes $\frac{20}{1}$.

2. Multiply the two fractions and reduce if necessary:

$$\frac{3}{4} \times \frac{20}{1} = \frac{3 \times 20}{4 \times 1} = \frac{60}{4} = 15$$

So $\frac{3}{4} \times 20 = 15$.

Fraction Sale!

Use a catalogue to go on an imaginary shopping spree and
practice multiplying whole numbers and fractions.

MATERIALS

catalogue
pencil
paper

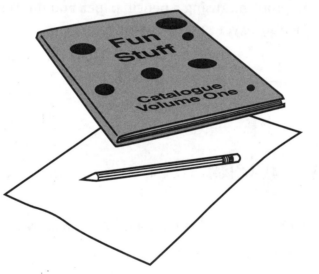

Procedure

1. Find a catalogue and make a list of items you would like to buy. Perhaps
you want a new sweater, a pair of jeans, and a CD player. How much do
the items on your list cost? Add them up.

2. Suppose everything in the catalogue were half price. To find the new
price, multiply the original price by $\frac{1}{2}$. For example, if a shirt costs $28,
multiply 28 by $\frac{1}{2}$ to find the new price:

$$28 \times \frac{1}{2} = \frac{28}{1} \times \frac{1}{2} = \frac{28 \times 1}{1 \times 2} = \frac{28}{2} = 14$$

How much do all of the items on your list cost now?

3. If everything in the catalogue were one-third off, how much would the items on your list cost? To find the new price, multiply the original price by $\frac{1}{3}$ to get the discount. Subtract the discount from the original price. Say one of the items on your list normally sells for $51. Multiply 51 by $\frac{1}{3}$:

$$51 \times \frac{1}{3} = \frac{51}{1} \times \frac{1}{3} = \frac{51 \times 1}{1 \times 3} = \frac{51}{3} = 17$$

Subtract the discount, $17, from the original price: 51 – 17 = 34. At one-third off, the item costs $34.

A faster method is to multiply 51 by $\frac{2}{3}$, since you are paying two-thirds of the original price:

$$51 \times \frac{2}{3} = \frac{51}{1} \times \frac{2}{3} = \frac{51 \times 2}{1 \times 3} = \frac{102}{3} = 34$$

Mixed-Number Products

Play this game to practice multiplying two mixed numbers.

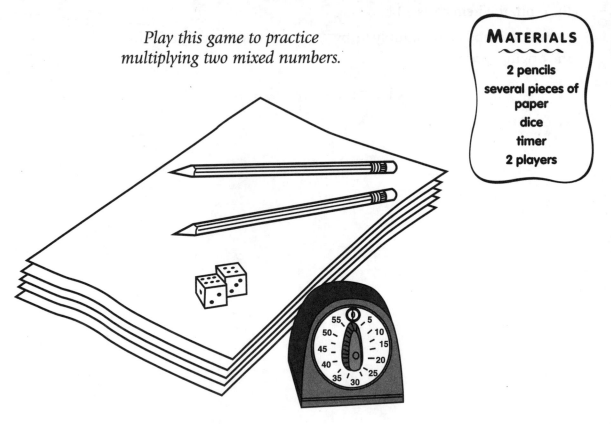

Game Rules

1. Player 1 writes a problem on a piece of paper for player 2 to solve. The problem should be a mixed number times a mixed number. The whole number in each mixed number can be any number from 1 to 5. The denominator can be any number from 2 to 8. A sample problem is $2\frac{7}{8} \times 5\frac{5}{6}$.

2. Player 1 places the paper facedown in front of player 2. Player 2 rolls the dice and multiplies the two numbers on the dice to find out how many seconds he or she has to solve the problem. For example, if the player rolls a 3 and a 4, he or she has 12 seconds to solve the problem.

3. When player 1 says, "Start," and starts the timer, player 2 turns the paper over and tries to solve the problem in the time allotted. Players may use a pencil, paper, and the Tips and Tricks box for help in multiplying mixed numbers.

4. When the time is up, player 1 says, "Stop." If player 2 solved the problem correctly in the time allotted, he or she earns 1 point.

5. Player 2 now writes a problem for player 1 to solve. The first player to earn 5 points wins the game.

SUPER MIXED-NUMBER PRODUCTS

Make the problems harder by using any number from 1 to 10 as the whole number and any number from 1 to 15 as the denominator in each mixed number.

Tips and Tricks

To multiply a mixed number by a mixed number, follow these three simple steps. The problem in this example is $3\frac{3}{8} \times 2\frac{1}{3}$.

1. Convert both mixed numbers to improper fractions. Remember to multiply the denominator by the whole number first; then add the product to the numerator.

$$3\frac{3}{8} = \frac{(8 \times 3) + 3}{8} = \frac{24 + 3}{8} = \frac{27}{8}$$

$$2\frac{1}{3} = \frac{(1 \times 2) + 1}{3} = \frac{6 + 1}{3} = \frac{7}{3}$$

2. Multiply the improper fractions:

$$\frac{27}{8} \times \frac{7}{3} = \frac{27 \times 7}{8 \times 3} = \frac{189}{24}$$

3. Reduce the fraction that is the product. If the fraction is improper, convert it to a mixed number.

$$\frac{189}{24} = \frac{63}{8} = 7\frac{7}{8}.$$

Add Them Up

*Use repeated addition to multiply
a whole number by a mixed number.*

MATERIALS

paper
pencil

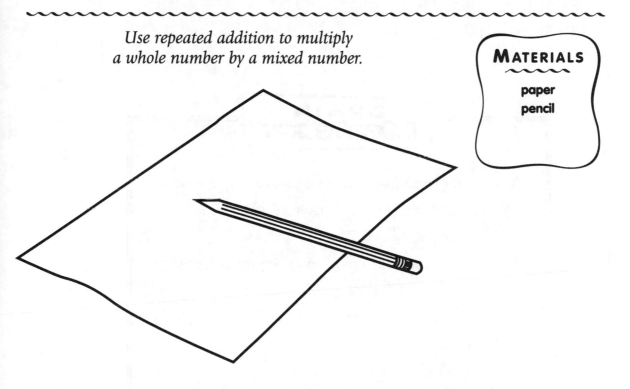

Procedure

1. Multiplication is repeated addition. Use this fact to solve multiplication problems. For example, what is $6 \times 3\frac{1}{2}$? Think of $6 \times 3\frac{1}{2}$ as six groups of $3\frac{1}{2}$. Here is how to add six groups of $3\frac{1}{2}$, or $3\frac{1}{2} + 3\frac{1}{2} + 3\frac{1}{2} + 3\frac{1}{2} + 3\frac{1}{2} + 3\frac{1}{2}$:

a. First add all the whole numbers: $3 + 3 + 3 + 3 + 3 + 3 = 18$.

b. Then add all the fractions: $\frac{1}{2} + \frac{1}{2} + \frac{1}{2} + \frac{1}{2} + \frac{1}{2} + \frac{1}{2} = \frac{6}{2}$.

c. Combine the sums: $18 + \frac{6}{2} = 18\frac{6}{2}$.

d. Reduce the fraction: $\frac{6}{2} = 3$. Then add it to the whole number: $3 + 18 = 21$. So $6 \times 3\frac{1}{2} = 21$.

2. Use repeated addition to solve these problems:

$3 \times 2\frac{1}{4}$

$2 \times \frac{3}{4}$

$3 \times 3\frac{1}{3}$

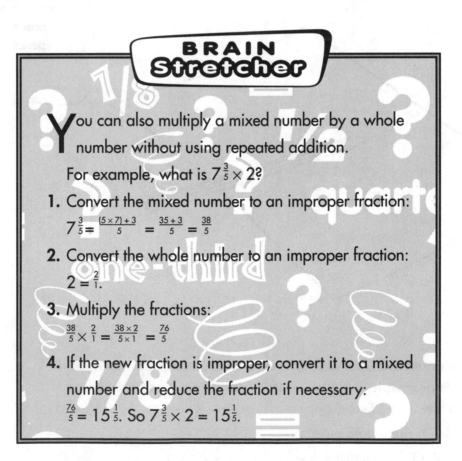

BRAIN Stretcher

You can also multiply a mixed number by a whole number without using repeated addition.

For example, what is $7\frac{3}{5} \times 2$?

1. Convert the mixed number to an improper fraction:

$$7\frac{3}{5} = \frac{(5 \times 7) + 3}{5} = \frac{35 + 3}{5} = \frac{38}{5}$$

2. Convert the whole number to an improper fraction: $2 = \frac{2}{1}$.

3. Multiply the fractions:

$$\frac{38}{5} \times \frac{2}{1} = \frac{38 \times 2}{5 \times 1} = \frac{76}{5}$$

4. If the new fraction is improper, convert it to a mixed number and reduce the fraction if necessary:

$$\frac{76}{5} = 15\frac{1}{5}. \text{ So } 7\frac{3}{5} \times 2 = 15\frac{1}{5}.$$

Domino Match

The "reciprocal" of a number is a number that can be
multiplied by the original number to give a product of 1. For
example, the reciprocal of 5, or $\frac{5}{1}$, is $\frac{1}{5}$, the reciprocal of $\frac{1}{2}$ is $\frac{2}{1}$,
or 2, and the reciprocal of $\frac{2}{3}$ is $\frac{3}{2}$. Play this game to practice
finding the reciprocal of a fraction.

MATERIALS

dominoes
2 pencils
21 index cards
several pieces of
paper
2 players

Game Preparation

1. Remove all the dominoes that are blank on one or both ends from the set.

2. Write one of the following numbers on each of 21 index cards:

1	4	$\frac{2}{2}$	$\frac{2}{5}$	$\frac{3}{4}$	$\frac{4}{4}$	$\frac{5}{5}$
2	5	$\frac{2}{3}$	$\frac{2}{6}$	$\frac{3}{5}$	$\frac{4}{5}$	$\frac{5}{6}$
3	6	$\frac{2}{4}$	$\frac{3}{3}$	$\frac{3}{6}$	$\frac{4}{6}$	$\frac{6}{6}$

Game Rules

1. Shuffle the cards and deal each player five cards. Place the rest of the cards facedown in a stack in the center of the table.

2. Place the dominoes facedown on the table and mix them up.

3. Player 1 turns over a domino. The dots on the domino represent the numerator and the denominator of two fractions. For example, if there are three dots on one end of the domino and five dots on the other end, the fractions are $\frac{3}{5}$ and $\frac{5}{3}$.

4. If the fraction on the domino, either upside down or right side up, is the reciprocal of the fraction or whole number on one of the cards in player 1's hand, he or she places the card on the table and the domino on top of the card. The player may discard only one of his or her cards in one turn. If the fraction is not the reciprocal, the player places the domino face-down on the table again. Players may use a pencil, paper, and the Tips and Tricks box for help in determining whether the fraction on the domino is the reciprocal of the fraction or whole number on the card.

5. Player 2 turns over a domino and determines whether the fraction on the domino is the reciprocal of the fraction or whole number on one of the cards in his or her hand. The first player to find the reciprocals of the fractions or whole numbers on all the cards in his or her hand wins the game.

Tips and Tricks

- ▼ To find the reciprocal of a fraction, switch the numerator and the denominator. The reciprocal of $\frac{3}{5}$ is $\frac{5}{3}$.

- ▼ To find the reciprocal of a whole number, first convert the number to a fraction by placing it over 1. Then switch the numerator and the denominator. The reciprocal of 5, or $\frac{5}{1}$, is $\frac{1}{5}$.

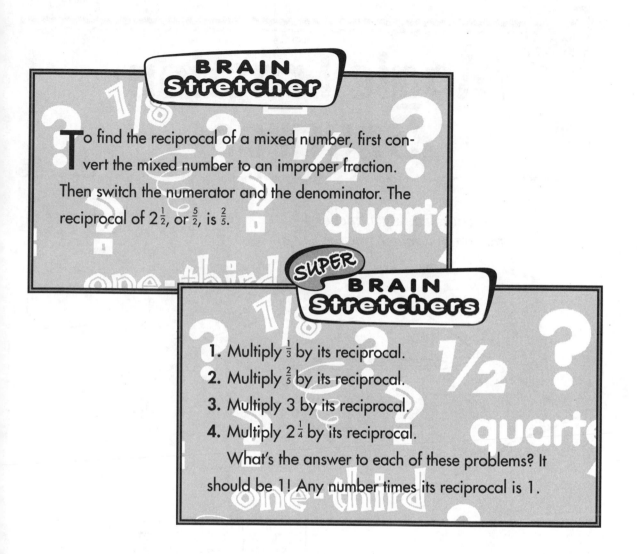

BRAIN Stretcher

To find the reciprocal of a mixed number, first convert the mixed number to an improper fraction. Then switch the numerator and the denominator. The reciprocal of $2\frac{1}{2}$, or $\frac{5}{2}$, is $\frac{2}{5}$.

SUPER BRAIN Stretchers

1. Multiply $\frac{1}{3}$ by its reciprocal.
2. Multiply $\frac{2}{5}$ by its reciprocal.
3. Multiply 3 by its reciprocal.
4. Multiply $2\frac{1}{4}$ by its reciprocal.

What's the answer to each of these problems? It should be 1! Any number times its reciprocal is 1.

30

Magic Fraction Squares

Practice dividing a fraction by a fraction in a magic fraction square.

MATERIALS

pencil
paper

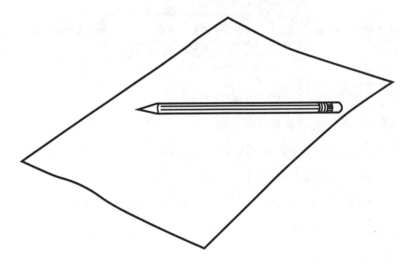

Procedure

1. Here is a magic fraction square. This square contains eight division problems and eight answers, or quotients. The quotients are in the corners.

$\frac{1}{2}$	$\frac{1}{2}$	$\frac{1}{4}$	2
$\frac{1}{3}$			$\frac{1}{8}$
$\frac{1}{6}$			$\frac{1}{4}$
2	$\frac{1}{10}$	$\frac{1}{5}$	$\frac{1}{2}$

2. Look at the top row. Skipping the left corner, the first problem is $\frac{1}{2} \div \frac{1}{4} = 2$. Here's how you solve the first problem. Note that $\frac{1}{4}$ is converted to its reciprocal, $\frac{4}{1}$, and the fractions are multiplied.

$$\frac{1}{2} \div \frac{1}{4} = \frac{1}{2} \times \frac{4}{1} = \frac{1 \times 4}{2 \times 1} = \frac{4}{2} = 2$$

Skipping the right corner, read the second problem, also in the top row, from right to left: $\frac{1}{4} \div \frac{1}{2} = \frac{1}{2}$. Here's how you solve the second problem. Again note that $\frac{1}{2}$ is converted to its reciprocal, $\frac{2}{1}$, and the fractions are multiplied.

$$\frac{1}{4} \div \frac{1}{2} = \frac{1}{4} \times \frac{2}{1} = \frac{1 \times 2}{4 \times 1} = \frac{2}{4} = \frac{1}{2}$$

3. Look at the left column. Skipping the top corner, read the third problem from top to bottom: $\frac{1}{3} \div \frac{1}{6} = 2$. Skipping the bottom corner, read the fourth problem from bottom to top: $\frac{1}{6} \div \frac{1}{3} = \frac{1}{2}$. How would you solve the third and fourth problems? You can use a pencil, paper, and the Tips and Tricks box for help in dividing a fraction by a fraction.

4. Look at the bottom row. Can you figure out the fifth and sixth problems and their quotients?

5. Look at the right column. Can you figure out the seventh and eighth problems and their quotients?

6. Here is another magic fraction square. Fill in the missing spaces. There is more than one right answer.

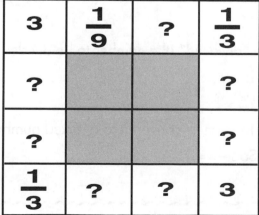

7. Can you solve this magic fraction square? There is no one right answer.

4	**?**	**?**	$\frac{1}{4}$
?			**?**
?			**?**
$\frac{1}{4}$	**?**	**?**	**4**

Tips and Tricks

To divide a fraction by a fraction, follow these three simple steps. The problem in this example is $\frac{1}{3} \div \frac{1}{4}$.

1. Find the reciprocal of the "divisor" (the number you are dividing by): The reciprocal of $\frac{1}{4}$ is $\frac{4}{1}$.

2. Multiply the "dividend" (the number to be divided), which is $\frac{1}{3}$, by the reciprocal of the divisor, $\frac{4}{1}$:

$\frac{1}{3} \times \frac{4}{1} = \frac{1 \times 4}{3 \times 1} = \frac{4}{3}$

3. Reduce the fraction or convert it to a mixed number if necessary:

$\frac{4}{3} = 1\frac{1}{3}$. So $\frac{1}{3} \div \frac{1}{4} = 1\frac{1}{3}$.

Look at these two problems:

1. What is $\frac{1}{2} \div \frac{1}{3}$?

2. What is $\frac{1}{3} \div \frac{1}{2}$?

The two problems do not have the same quotient. In multiplication, problems are "commutative." You get the same product no matter what order the numbers to be multiplied are in. Division is *not* commutative. The order of the problem *does* matter.

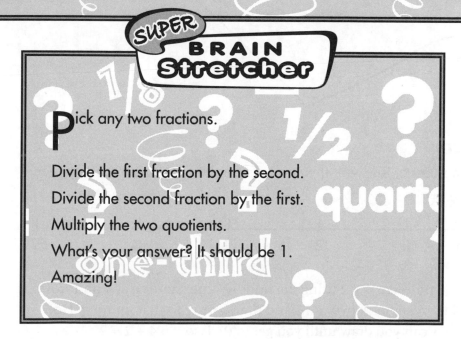

Pick any two fractions.

Divide the first fraction by the second.

Divide the second fraction by the first.

Multiply the two quotients.

What's your answer? It should be 1.

Amazing!

31

Number Line Division

Learn how to use a number line to divide a whole number by a fraction.

MATERIALS

pencil
paper

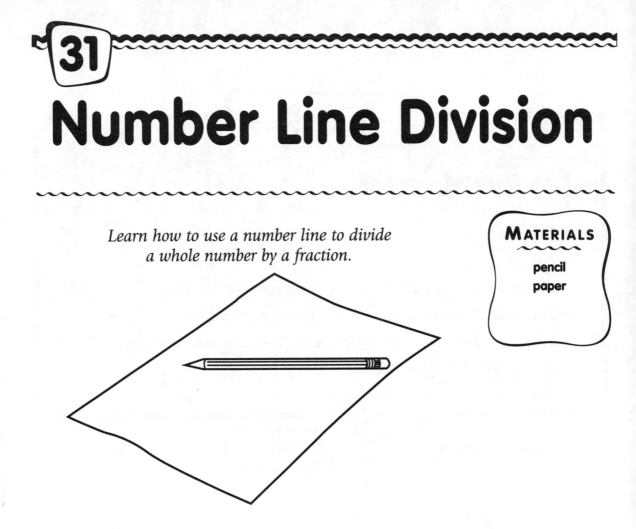

Procedure

1. Draw a number line with the numbers from 0 to 5 on a piece of paper.

2. Solve the problem 4 ÷ 2 using the number line. Starting at 4 and working toward 0, count back two units and draw an arc to that number. How many arcs can you draw until you get to 0? Two. So 4 ÷ 2 = 2.

3. Draw a new number line with the numbers from 0 to 5 and all the halves in between. Solve the problem $4 \div \frac{1}{2}$ using this number line.

Start at 4 and draw semi-circles, counting back half a unit at a time until you get to 0. How many arcs did you draw?

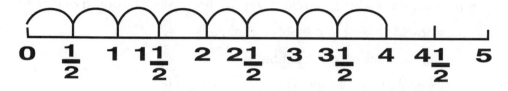

4. What is $3 \div \frac{1}{3}$? Draw a new number line with the numbers from 0 to 5 and the thirds in between. Start at 3 and draw arcs, counting back one-third of a unit at a time until you get to 0. How many semi-circles can you draw until you get to 0?

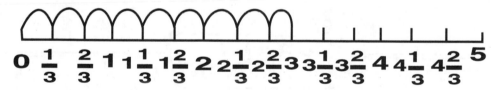

5. What is $2 \div \frac{2}{3}$? Draw another number line numbered from 0 to 5 in thirds. Start at 2 and draw semi-circles, counting back two-thirds of a unit at a time until you get to 0. How many semi-circles can you draw until you get to 0?

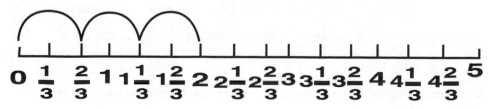

6. Use number lines to divide these whole numbers by these fractions.

$3 \div \frac{1}{2}$

$6 \div \frac{3}{4}$

$1 \div \frac{1}{2}$

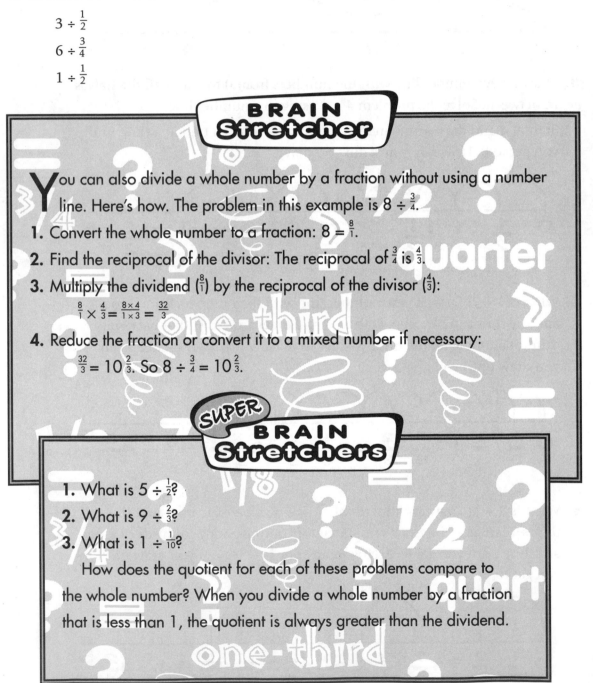

BRAIN Stretcher

You can also divide a whole number by a fraction without using a number line. Here's how. The problem in this example is $8 \div \frac{3}{4}$.

1. Convert the whole number to a fraction: $8 = \frac{8}{1}$.

2. Find the reciprocal of the divisor: The reciprocal of $\frac{3}{4}$ is $\frac{4}{3}$.

3. Multiply the dividend ($\frac{8}{1}$) by the reciprocal of the divisor ($\frac{4}{3}$):

$$\frac{8}{1} \times \frac{4}{3} = \frac{8 \times 4}{1 \times 3} = \frac{32}{3}$$

4. Reduce the fraction or convert it to a mixed number if necessary:

$$\frac{32}{3} = 10\frac{2}{3}. \text{ So } 8 \div \frac{3}{4} = 10\frac{2}{3}.$$

SUPER BRAIN Stretchers

1. What is $5 \div \frac{1}{2}$?

2. What is $9 \div \frac{2}{3}$?

3. What is $1 \div \frac{1}{10}$?

How does the quotient for each of these problems compare to the whole number? When you divide a whole number by a fraction that is less than 1, the quotient is always greater than the dividend.

32

Shoe Box Fractions

*Play a game on a shoe box lid to
practice dividing a fraction by a whole number.*

MATERIALS

20 index cards
pencil
shoe box lid
marker
die
2 players

Game Preparation

1. On five of the index cards, write "All Play." Leave the other 15 cards
   blank. Put all the cards together in a stack so that the words "All Play" are
   facedown.

2. Turn the shoe box lid over so that the inside of the lid is faceup. Use a
   marker to draw the grid shown here on the inside of the lid. The grid
   should fill up the entire lid.

$\dfrac{1}{6}$	$\dfrac{1}{3}$	$\dfrac{2}{3}$
$\dfrac{1}{4}$	$\dfrac{3}{4}$	$\dfrac{1}{5}$
$\dfrac{2}{5}$	$\dfrac{1}{2}$	$\dfrac{3}{8}$
$\dfrac{5}{8}$	$\dfrac{1}{8}$	$\dfrac{3}{5}$
$\dfrac{7}{8}$	$\dfrac{4}{5}$	$\dfrac{5}{8}$

Game Rules

1. Shuffle the cards and place them facedown in the center of the table.

2. Player 1 rolls the die so that it lands somewhere on the grid. The fraction the die lands on is the dividend of a problem and the number on the die is the divisor. For example, if the die lands on $\frac{1}{2}$ and the player rolled a 3, then the problem is $\frac{1}{2} \div 3$.

3. Player 1 picks up the top card and turns it faceup. If the card is blank, he or she alone solves the problem. But if the player draws an All Play card, then both players try to solve the problem. Players may not use a pencil and paper to solve the problem, but they may use the Tips and Tricks box for help. The first player to shout out the correct answer earns 1 point. If a player calls out an incorrect answer, the other player earns the point.

4. Player 2 takes a turn. The first player to earn 10 points wins the game.

Tips and Tricks

To divide a fraction by a whole number, follow these four simple steps. The problem in this example is $\frac{3}{5} \div 9$.

1. Convert the whole number (which is the divisor) to a fraction by placing it over 1: $9 = \frac{9}{1}$.

2. Find the reciprocal of the divisor: The reciprocal of $\frac{9}{1}$ is $\frac{1}{9}$.

3. Multiply the dividend by the reciprocal of the divisor: $\frac{3}{5} \times \frac{1}{9} = \frac{3 \times 1}{5 \times 9} = \frac{3}{45}$

4. Reduce the fraction if necessary: $\frac{3}{45} = \frac{1}{15}$.
   So $\frac{3}{5} \div 9 = \frac{1}{15}$.

SUPER SHOE BOX FRACTIONS

In Super Shoe Box Fractions, players divide a mixed number by a mixed number. Two dice are rolled. The number on each die is the whole number of a mixed number, and the fraction the die lands on is the fraction of the mixed number. For example, if the first die rolled is a 5 and it lands on $\frac{1}{2}$, then the first mixed number is $5\frac{1}{2}$, and it is the dividend. If the second die rolled is a 2 and it lands on $\frac{1}{3}$, then the second mixed number is $2\frac{1}{3}$, and it is the divisor. The problem is $5\frac{1}{2} \div 2\frac{1}{3}$. Players may use only the Advanced Tips and Tricks box for help.

Tips and Tricks

To divide a mixed number by a mixed number, follow these four simple steps. The problem in the example is $2\frac{2}{3} \div 1\frac{1}{2}$.

1. Convert both mixed numbers to improper fractions:

$$2\frac{2}{3} = \frac{(3 \times 2) + 2}{3} = \frac{6 + 2}{3} = \frac{8}{3}$$

$$1\frac{1}{2} = \frac{(2 \times 1) + 1}{2} = \frac{2 + 1}{2} = \frac{3}{2}$$

2. Find the reciprocal of the divisor: The reciprocal of $\frac{3}{2}$ is $\frac{2}{3}$.

3. Multiply the dividend by the reciprocal of the divisor:

$$\frac{8}{3} \times \frac{2}{3} = \frac{8 \times 2}{3 \times 3} = \frac{16}{9}$$

4. Reduce the fraction or convert it to a mixed number if necessary:

$\frac{16}{9} = 1\frac{7}{9}$. So $2\frac{2}{3} \div 1\frac{1}{2} = 1\frac{7}{9}$.

33

Three-in-a Row Bingo

Practice adding, subtracting, multiplying, and dividing fractions.

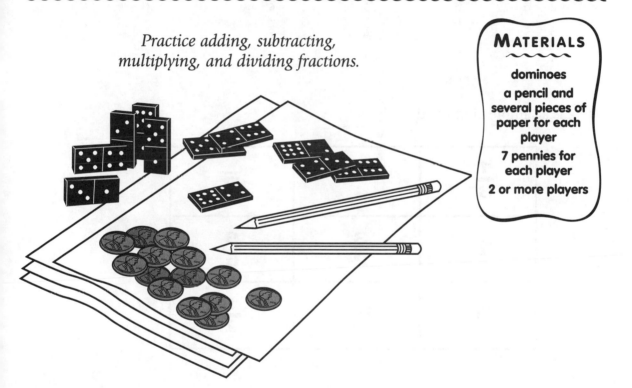

Game Preparation

Remove all the dominoes that are blank on one or both ends from the set.

Game Rules

1. Spread the remaining dominoes facedown on the table.
2. Each player draws a three-by-three grid on a piece of paper.

3. Each player writes one of the following whole numbers or fractions in each of the squares to create a bingo card such as the one shown. The player can choose any nine numbers and place them on the card wherever he or she wants.

1	5	$\frac{1}{4}$	$\frac{3}{4}$	$\frac{4}{3}$
2	6	$\frac{1}{5}$	$\frac{5}{6}$	$\frac{5}{4}$
3	$\frac{1}{2}$	$\frac{1}{6}$	$\frac{7}{6}$	$\frac{6}{5}$
4	$\frac{1}{3}$	$\frac{2}{3}$	$\frac{3}{2}$	0

Here is a sample bingo card.

$\frac{1}{3}$	$\frac{3}{4}$	5
1	$\frac{3}{2}$	$\frac{6}{5}$
0	$\frac{4}{3}$	$\frac{1}{2}$

4. Player 1 turns over two dominoes and makes two fractions from each domino. A total of four fractions are made. The player then takes as long as he or she needs to add, subtract, multiply, and divide pairs of the fractions, seeing if any of the answers match any number on his or her bingo card. If player 1 finds a match, he or she uses a penny to cover the number. Players may cover only one number on the card per turn. Suppose a player draws two dominoes that look like the ones shown.

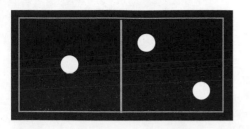 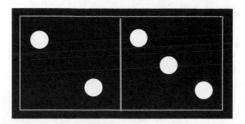

From these two dominoes, four fractions can be made:

$$\frac{1}{2} \qquad \frac{2}{1} \qquad \frac{2}{3} \qquad \frac{3}{2}.$$

Since $\frac{3}{2} - \frac{1}{2} = \frac{2}{2} = 1$, the player can cover the number 1 on his or her bingo card. Other combinations of two fractions from above should be added, subtracted, multiplied, or divided until an answer matches a number on the card, if possible.

5. Player 2 turns over two dominoes and sees if he or she can make up a problem whose answer matches any number on his or her bingo card. The first player to cover three numbers in a row wins the game.

V

FRACTIONS, DECIMALS, AND MORE

You might think you know all about fractions now that you know how to add, subtract, multiply, and divide fractions, but there is still more to learn. "Decimals" are fractions, too, and in this section you will learn how to change a fraction to a decimal and a decimal to a fraction. You'll solve a crossword puzzle, connect the dots, do a word search, and play a noisy game of Order, all while learning about fractions and decimals. You will become so fabulous with fractions that you'll amaze your friends and teachers. When you're done, you'll be a fractions master.

3/4   98.2
2/3   7.25
8.50   26.2
5/8   1½
5.0   1/4

Order

Play this noisy game to learn how to put fractions in order from smallest to largest.

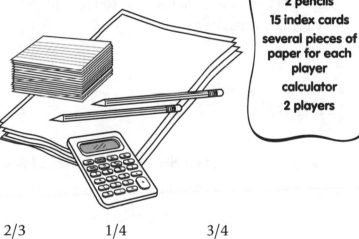

Game Preparation

Write one of the following fractions on each of 15 index cards:

1/2	1/3	2/3	1/4	3/4
1/6	5/6	1/8	3/8	5/8
7/8	1/12	5/12	7/12	11/12

Game Rules

1. Shuffle the cards and deal each player five cards. Place the remaining cards facedown in a stack in the center of the table.

2. Each player places his or her cards facedown in a row in front of himself or herself.

3. One player shouts, "Ready, set, go!" and both players turn over their cards and try to put them in order from the smallest fraction (only one on each card) to the largest.

4. When a player thinks his or her fractions are in the correct order, he or she shouts, "Done!"

5. To check the order of the fractions, find a common denominator. When all five fractions have a common denominator, compare the numerators to make sure they are in order. Players may use a calculator and the Tips and Tricks box for help in determining the order. If the first player to finish is correct, he or she wins the round. If the player is incorrect, the other player wins the round.

6. All the cards are returned to a single pile and shuffled. Each player is again dealt five cards and a second round is played. The first player to win three rounds wins the game.

Tips and Tricks

To convert a fraction to a decimal using a calculator, follow these three simple steps. The fraction in this example is 5/12.

1. Enter the numerator 5 into the calculator. Then press the division key.

2. Enter the denominator 12 into the calculator. Then press the enter or equals key.

3. The number 0.42 appears on the screen. This is the decimal equivalent of 5/12.

To convert several fractions to decimals and put them in order, write the decimal of each fraction on a piece of paper. Put the decimals in order from smallest to largest. The order of the decimals is the order of their equivalent fractions.

SUPER ORDER

Make a new set of cards with the following fractions on them:

1/2	1/3	2/3	1/4	3/4	1/5	2/5	3/5	4/5	1/6	5/6
1/7	2/7	3/7	4/7	5/7	6/7	1/8	3/8	5/8	7/8	1/9
2/9	4/9	5/9	6/9	7/9	8/9	1/10	3/10	7/10	9/10	1/12
5/12	7/12	11/12	1/15	2/15	4/15	7/15	8/15	11/15	13/15	14/15

Play Super Order with this new deck of cards.

ORDER SOLITAIRE

Shuffle a deck of fraction cards and turn over the first five cards. Use a stop-watch to time how long it takes you to put the fractions on the cards in order from smallest to largest. Write down your time. Turn over the next five cards and put them in order from smallest to largest. See if you can beat your previous time.

35

Dancing Decimals

Convert a decimal to a fraction in three easy steps.

MATERIALS

playing cards
pencil
index card
paper

Procedure

1. Remove all the face cards (kings, queens, and jacks) from a deck of playing cards. Shuffle the cards and place them facedown in a stack to your right.

2. Write a zero and a decimal point (0.) on an index card.

3. Place the index card faceup in front of you.

4. Use one playing card to make a decimal in tenths and convert it to a fraction.

    a. Turn over the top playing card and place it to the right of the decimal point. The number on the playing card and the decimal point make a decimal in tenths. For example, if you turn over the 5 of spades, the decimal is 0.5.

    b. Write this decimal on a piece of paper and convert it to a fraction. The numerator is the number on the playing card. The denominator is 10. So 0.5 becomes 5/10.

    c. Reduce the fraction if necessary: 5/10 = 1/2.

5. Put aside the playing card from step 4. Turn over two more cards and place them to the right of the decimal point. These two playing cards make a decimal in hundredths. Say you turn over the 2 of hearts and the 5 of diamonds. The decimal is 0.25. Convert the decimal to a fraction in which the numerator is 25 and the denominator is 100. So 0.25 becomes 25/100. Reduce the fraction: 25/100 = 1/4.

6. Put aside the playing cards from step 5. Turn over three more playing cards and place them to the right of the decimal point. These three playing cards make a decimal in thousandths. Can you figure out how to convert the decimal to a fraction?

When you convert a decimal to a fraction, the denominator of the fraction is a multiple of 10, such as 10 for tenths, 100 for hundredths, 1,000 for thousandths, 10,000 for ten-thousandths, and so on. How do you know whether to use 10, 100, 1,000, or any other multiple of 10? Just count the number of places to the right of the decimal point. This is the number of 0's to use in the denominator. For example:

0.8 = 8/10
0.08 = 8/100
0.008 = 8/1,000
0.0008 = 8/10,000

36

Fraction *Jeopardy!*

Practice your fraction skills while playing Fraction Jeopardy!

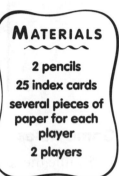

MATERIALS

2 pencils
25 index cards
several pieces of paper for each player
2 players

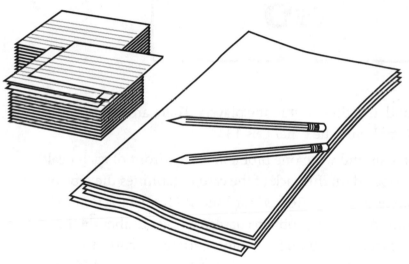

Game Preparation

1. On the back of five index cards, write "Lowest Terms."

2. On the back of five other index cards, write "Addition of Fractions."

3. On the back of five other index cards, write "Subtraction of Fractions."

4. On the back of five other index cards, write "Multiplication of Fractions."

5. On the back of five other index cards, write "Division of Fractions."

6. Below the words on each set of cards, write one of the following numbers on each card:

       10   20   30   40   50

For example, in the Multiplication of Fractions set, one card should have a 10, one a 20, one a 30, one a 40, and one a 50. Set up each set this way. A sample card is shown here.

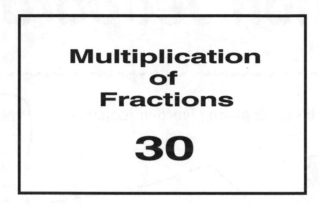

Game Rules

1. Shuffle the cards and deal them out to the players. There are 25 cards, so one player gets 12 cards and the other gets 13.

2. Players create problems and write one problem on the front of each dealt card. The category labeled on the back of the card determines the type of problem. For example, a "Lowest Terms" card should have a fraction to reduce. Vary the difficulty of the problems based on the number on the back of the card, which is the number of points earned for correctly solving the problem. Cards with higher numbers should have more difficult problems, while cards with lower numbers should have easier problems. A level 20 problem on an Addition of Fractions card is shown.

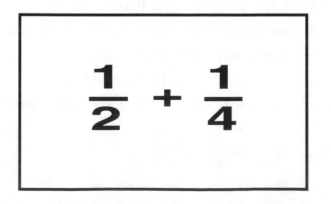

3. Place all the cards on the table so that the problems are facedown. Arrange the cards in five columns and five rows according to category and point value. Put the Lowest Terms cards in column 1, Addition of Fractions cards in column 2, Subtraction of Fractions cards in column 3, Multiplication of Fractions cards in column 4, and Division of Fractions cards in column 5. Put the 10-point cards in row 1, 20-point cards in row 2, 30-point cards in row 3, 40-point cards in row 4, and 50-point cards in row 5 as shown.

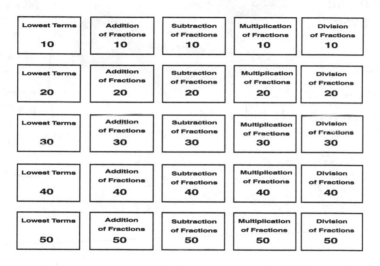

4. Player 1 turns over any card, and both players try to solve the problem. The first player to correctly solve the problem keeps the card and turns over another card. Both players try to solve this new problem. If a player solves a problem incorrectly, that player must give one of the cards he or she has won, of equal or greater value, to the other player.

5. The game continues until all cards have been played. At the end of the game, players add up the points on the back of their cards. The player with the most points wins.

SUPER FRACTION *JEOPARDY!*

Make 25 new cards with harder problems that award point values of 20, 40, 60, 80, and 100.

Problem Generator

Practice working with fractions by creating fractions

Game Preparation

Write one of the following
fractional expressions on each of 15 index cards:

$\frac{1}{2}$	$\frac{7}{12}$	$\frac{4}{3}$	1	$3\frac{1}{4}$
$\frac{3}{4}$	$\frac{7}{8}$	$\frac{17}{12}$	5	$4\frac{2}{3}$
$\frac{1}{25}$	$\frac{9}{2}$	7	$2\frac{1}{2}$	$6\frac{5}{6}$

Game Rules

1. Shuffle the cards and place them facedown in the center of the table.

2. Player 1 turns over the top card, and player 2 starts the timer. Player 1 has 3 minutes to create as many fraction problems as he or she can in which the fraction on the card is the answer to the problem. The player must create an addition problem, a subtraction problem, a multiplication problem, and a division problem in that order. When the player has created four problems in this order, he or she can create four new problems in the same order. Players may use only a pencil and paper to create the problems. When 3 minutes is up, the player earns 1 point for each correct problem.

3. Player 2 turns over the top card and creates as many problems as he or she can in 3 minutes. The player with the most points after three rounds is the winner.

Crossword Puzzle

Convert fractions to decimals to solve a crossword puzzle.

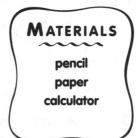

MATERIALS

pencil
paper
calculator

Procedure

1. To convert a fraction to a decimal, divide the numerator by the denominator. For example, to convert $\frac{3}{5}$ to a decimal, divide 3 by 5. Place a decimal point and as many 0's as necessary after the dividend (3) until it is evenly divided.

$$
\begin{array}{r}
0.6 \\
5 \overline{)\ 3.0} \\
-3.0 \\
\hline
0
\end{array}
$$

2. These fractions are clues to the crossword puzzle. The puzzle can be solved by converting the fractions to decimals.

Across

1. $\frac{3}{4}$
3. $\frac{1}{2}$
5. $\frac{3}{10}$
7. $207\frac{32}{100}$
9. $3\frac{1}{2}$
10. $\frac{75}{100}$
11. $\frac{1}{5}$

Down

1. $\frac{1}{8}$
2. $5\frac{7}{10}$
4. $5\frac{1}{4}$
6. $3\frac{3}{8}$
8. $3\frac{1}{2}$

3. Create your own crossword puzzle of fraction-to-decimal problems. Use a pencil, paper, and a calculator to make up the clues and the solution.

BRAIN Stretcher

What do you do when you divide the numerator of a fraction by the denominator and the decimal repeats? Watch what happens when you convert $\frac{1}{3}$ to a decimal:

The dividend (1) will never divide evenly. What do you do? Write three dots after the quotient, or 0.3333 . . . , to indicate that the number 3 continuously repeats itself. This type of decimal is called a "repeating decimal." Another way to write a repeating decimal is $0.3\overline{3}$, with a bar over the last 3. The bar means the 3 repeats.

$$
\begin{array}{r}
0.3333 \\
3\overline{)1.0000} \\
-9 \\
\hline
10 \\
-9 \\
\hline
10 \\
-9 \\
\hline
10 \\
-9 \\
\hline
1
\end{array}
$$

Challenging Dot-to-Dot

Challenge your fractions skills while you solve a dot-to-dot picture puzzle.

MATERIALS

pencil
paper
calculator

Procedure

1. Copy the dot-to-dot puzzle on a piece of paper.
2. Convert the fractions to decimals.
3. Starting at 0, connect the dots in order from smallest decimal to largest. An interesting picture is revealed.

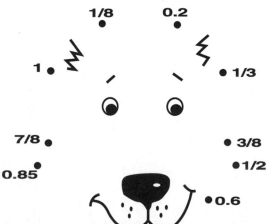

0

1/4

1/8   **0.2**

1.   **1/3**

7/8   **3/8**

0.85   **1/2**

0.6

3/4   **2/3**

5/8

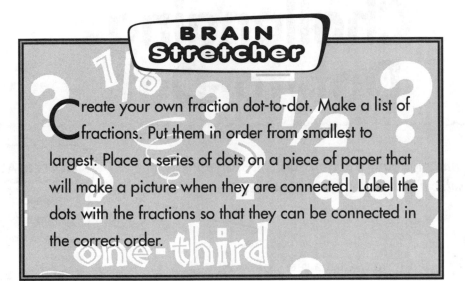

BRAIN Stretcher

Create your own fraction dot-to-dot. Make a list of fractions. Put them in order from smallest to largest. Place a series of dots on a piece of paper that will make a picture when they are connected. Label the dots with the fractions so that they can be connected in the correct order.

Fraction Words

Find fraction words in this word search puzzle.

MATERIALS

pencil
paper

Procedure

Fourteen mathematical terms relating to fractions and at least two fun terms are hidden in this grid. The words can be arranged horizontally, vertically, or diagonally, and forward or backward. Make a photocopy of the grid. Find the words and circle them with your pencil.

X	Z	O	P	R	S	R	O	T	A	R	E	M	U	N
U	Y	I	M	D	V	H	R	R	E	N	D	I	O	E
J	Y	Q	I	S	P	N	E	F	A	O	I	M	P	X
M	H	W	X	A	L	Y	C	V	E	I	L	P	I	C
M	N	D	E	N	O	M	I	N	A	T	O	R	N	E
T	B	E	D	O	M	U	P	V	S	C	W	O	E	L
N	V	R	N	E	M	I	R	P	W	A	E	P	E	L
E	F	I	U	I	O	P	O	D	S	R	S	E	L	E
L	R	T	M	L	O	L	C	M	D	F	T	R	P	N
A	Z	Y	B	P	P	O	A	X	R	B	T	B	I	T
V	A	G	E	B	J	I	L	Z	S	A	E	A	T	W
I	Q	F	R	Q	Q	I	R	E	P	O	R	P	L	O
U	S	H	T	R	U	O	F	S	W	R	M	E	U	R
Q	X	B	I	R	V	A	S	Y	S	O	S	E	M	K
E	C	U	D	E	R	L	L	S	X	P	B	T	I	Z

FRACTIONS MASTER CERTIFICATE

Now that you've mastered all the fraction facts, problems, and games in this book, you are officially certified as a fractions master! Make a photocopy of this certificate, write your name on the copy, and hang it on the wall.

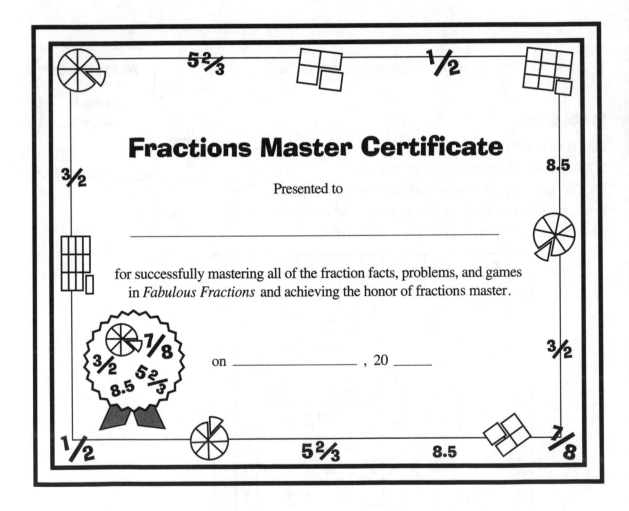

Fractions Master Certificate

Presented to

_____

for successfully mastering all of the fraction facts, problems, and games in *Fabulous Fractions* and achieving the honor of fractions master.

on _____ , 20 _____

Index